W9-AZL-575

REVELATION
UNVEILING THE END

ACT 2

The EARTHLY *Drama*

FROM THE BIBLE-TEACHING MINISTRY OF
CHARLES R. SWINDOLL

INSIGHT FOR LIVING

REVELATION—UNVEILING THE END, ACT 2
The Earthly Drama

Bible Companion

FROM THE BIBLE-TEACHING MINISTRY OF CHARLES R. SWINDOLL

Charles R. Swindoll has devoted his life to the clear, practical teaching and application of God's Word and His grace. A pastor at heart, Chuck has served as senior pastor to congregations in Texas, Massachusetts, and California. He currently pastors Stonebriar Community Church in Frisco, Texas, but Chuck's listening audience extends far beyond a local church body. As a leading program in Christian broadcasting, *Insight for Living* airs in major Christian radio markets around the world, reaching people groups in languages they can understand. Chuck's extensive writing ministry has also served the body of Christ worldwide and his leadership as president and now chancellor of Dallas Theological Seminary has helped prepare and equip a new generation for ministry. Chuck and Cynthia, his partner in life and ministry, have four grown children and ten grandchildren

Based on the original outlines, charts, and transcripts of Charles R. Swindoll's sermons, the Bible Companion text was developed and written by Michael J. Svigel, Th.M., Ph.D. candidate, Dallas Theological Seminary.

Editor in Chief: Cynthia Swindoll, President, Insight for Living
Executive Vice President: Wayne Stiles, Th.M., D.Min., Dallas Theological Seminary
Editor: Brie Engeler, B.A., University Scholars, Baylor University
Copy Editor: Jim Craft, M.A., English, Mississippi College
Proofreaders: Melissa Carlisle, M.A., Christian Education, Dallas Theological Seminary
        Mike Penn, B.A., Journalism, University of Oklahoma
Cover Designer: Steven Tomlin, Embry-Riddle Aeronautical University, 1992–1995
Production Artist: Nancy Gustine, B.F.A., Advertising Art, University of North Texas
Cover Images: Sky photo—Comstock, Inc.
        Olive branch—Alex Slobodkin
        Jerusalem photo—Todd Bolen/BiblePlaces.com

Published by IFL Publishing House, A Division of Insight for Living
Post Office Box 251007, Plano, Texas 75025-1007

Unless otherwise identified, Scripture quotations are from the *New American Standard Bible*® (NASB). Copyright © 1960, 1962, 1963, 1968, 1971, 1972, 1973, 1975, 1977, 1995 by The Lockman Foundation, La Habra, California. All rights reserved. Used by permission. (www.Lockman.org)

Scripture quotations marked (MSG) are taken from *THE MESSAGE*. Copyright © 1993, 1994, 1995, 1996, 2000, 2001, 2002 by Eugene H. Peterson. All rights reserved. Used by permission of NavPress Publishing Group.

Scripture quotations marked (NLT) are taken from the *Holy Bible, New Living Translation*. Copyright © 1996 by Tyndale House Publishers, Inc., Wheaton, Illinois 60189 USA. All rights reserved. Used by permission.

An effort has been made to locate sources and obtain permission where necessary for the quotations used in this Bible Companion. In the event of any unintentional omission, a modification will gladly be incorporated in future printings.

ISBN: 978-1-57972-723-9
Printed in the United States of America

TABLE OF CONTENTS

A Letter from Chuck

Like a classic cliffhanger, the first act of the book of Revelation concluded with unrelieved anticipation. When the Lamb of God took the seven-sealed scroll from the Almighty, all creation broke forth in resounding praise that reverberated to the very foundations of the earth (Revelation 5:8–14). Yet as soon as His finger reached to pluck the first seal from that scroll, the curtains swept across the heavenly stage, leaving the audience seated in silent awe.

Welcome to the second act of the book of Revelation—God's age-old saga of judgment and redemption. In this installment of our end-times trilogy, we will witness the rapid-fire unfolding of an intense, earthly drama through the vivid descriptions of the apostle John. The four horsemen of the Apocalypse begin their gallop; seven trumpets announce cataclysmic catastrophe; saints, witnesses, and martyrs stand together against incomprehensible adversaries; and all the powers of Satan concentrate in the ultimate evil empire ruled by the infamous Antichrist.

Yet from these shocking end-times visions, eternal truths about God, humanity, judgment, and salvation emerge. Jesus Christ stands at the center as coming Judge and King, meting out justice and wrath while extending mercy and grace. When you step into the startling visions of Revelation 6–13 with the expectation that God is working in our lives today, His words will not merely *inform* you, they will *transform* you.

So take your seat. The houselights are dimming. The curtain is parting. The earthly drama is about to begin . . .

Charles R. Swindoll

HOW TO USE THIS BIBLE COMPANION

Welcome to *Revelation—Unveiling the End, Act 2*. In this exciting second installment of God's earthly drama, we continue our journey into the heart of the book
of Revelation. No other book of the Bible—nor any part of history—has evoked
greater fascination and controversy than this book of visions, symbols, and images. This study will help you to understand John's visions in the context of your
life—and you will truly be changed. Many people forget that the truth communi-
cated in the book of Revelation is not just something to be studied; it is something
to be *lived*. This Bible Companion will help you do both.

A brief introduction to the overall structure of each lesson will help you get
the most out of these studies, whether you choose to complete this study indi-
vidually or as part of a group.

LESSON ORGANIZATION

 Each of the thirteen lessons begins with **THE HEART OF THE MATTER**,
which highlights the main idea of the lesson. The lesson itself is then
composed of three main teaching sections—"You Are Here," "Discovering the Way," and "Starting Your Journey."

 YOU ARE HERE includes an introduction and thought-provoking
questions to orient you to the topic that will be examined in the lesson.

 DISCOVERING THE WAY explores the principles of Scripture
through observation and interpretation of Bible passages and
drawing out practical principles for life. Parallel passages and additional
questions supplement the main Scriptures for more in-depth study.

STARTING YOUR JOURNEY focuses on application to help you put into practice the principles of the lesson in ways that fit your personality, gifts, and level of spiritual maturity.

USING THE BIBLE COMPANION

Revelation—Unveiling the End, Act 2 Bible Companion is designed with both individual study and small-group use in mind. Here's the method we recommend:

Prayer—Begin each lesson with prayer, asking God to teach you through His Word and to open your heart to the self-discovery afforded by the questions and text of the lesson.

Scripture—Have your Bible handy. We recommend the New American Standard Bible or another literal translation, rather than a paraphrase. As you progress through each lesson, you'll be prompted to read relevant sections of Scripture and answer questions related to the topic. You will also want to look up Scripture passages noted in parentheses.

Questions—As you encounter the questions, approach them wisely and creatively. Not every question will be applicable to each person all the time. If you can't answer a question, continue on in the lesson. Use the questions as general guides in your thinking rather than rigid forms to complete. If there are things you just don't understand or that you want to explore further, be sure to jot down your thoughts or questions.

Features—Throughout the chapters, you'll find several special features designed to add insight or depth to your study. Use these features to enhance your study and deepen your knowledge of Scripture, history, and theology. An explanation of each feature can be found beginning on page xi.

A SPECIAL NOTE FOR SMALL GROUPS

If you have chosen to complete this study in a small-group format, carefully consider the following suggestions:

Preparation—All group members should try to prepare in advance by working through the lessons as described in the previous section. If you serve as the leader, you should take additional steps to supplement your preparation either by listening to the corresponding sermons (available for purchase at www.insight.org) or by reading any of the recommended resources. Mastery of the material will build your confidence and competence, and approaching the topic from various perspectives will equip you to freely guide discussion.

Discussion Questions—You should feel free to mold the lesson according to the needs of your unique group. At a minimum, however, the group should cover the questions marked by the group icons in each of the three main sections during your meeting time. While planning the lesson, you will want to mark additional questions you feel fit the time allotment, needs, and interests of your group. The questions are divided to assist you in your lesson preparation. Note that series of questions marked by the clock icon are *primary*—meant to contribute to a solid understanding of the lesson. The unmarked series of questions are *secondary*—intended to provide a deeper exploration of the topic and corresponding Scripture passages. Encourage your group members to dig into these questions on their own.

Flexibility—During group time, open in prayer, then lead the group through the lesson you planned in advance. Members may want to share their own answers to the questions, contribute their insights, or steer the discussion in a particular direction that fits the needs of the group. Sometimes group members will want to discuss questions you may have left out of the planned lesson. *Be flexible*, but try to stay on schedule so the group has sufficient time for the final section, "Starting Your Journey," where the application of the lesson begins.

Goal—If it's unrealistic for your group to complete a single lesson during a session, consider continuing where you left off in the next session. The goal is not merely to cover material but to promote in-depth, personal discussion of the topic with a view toward personal response and application. To do this, the group will need to both understand the biblical principles and apply them to their lives.

Our prayer is that the biblical principles, exercises, and applications in this Bible Companion will help you not only to understand the meaning of the book of Revelation but also to apply the truth it contains to your life.

SPECIAL BIBLE COMPANION FEATURES

Lessons are supplemented with a variety of special features to summarize and clarify teaching points or to provide opportunities for more advanced study. Although they are not essential for understanding and applying the principles in the lesson, they will offer valuable nuggets of insight as you work through this material.

 GETTING TO THE ROOT
While our English versions of the Scriptures are reliable, studying the original languages can often bring to light nuances of the text that are sometimes missed in translation. This feature explores the meaning of the underlying Hebrew or Greek words or phrases in a particular passage, sometimes providing parallel examples to illuminate the meaning of the inspired text.

 DIGGING DEEPER
Various passages in Scripture touch on deeper theological questions or confront modern worldviews and philosophies that conflict with a biblical worldview. This feature will help you gain deeper insight into specific theological issues related to the biblical text.

 DOORWAY TO HISTORY
Sometimes the chronological gap that separates us from the original author and readers clouds our understanding of a passage of Scripture. This feature takes you back in time to explore the surrounding history, culture, and customs of the world in which Revelation was written.

REVELATION
UNVEILING THE END

ACT 2

The EARTHLY *Drama*

LET THE JUDGMENTS BEGIN

Revelation 6:1–8

THE HEART OF THE MATTER

When the heavenly stage was set in Revelation 1–5, John visited the throne room of God, falling down with angels and saints in worship and singing with a choir of countless creatures in heaven and on earth: "Worthy is the Lamb!" But now, with the beginning of Revelation 6, the scene changes dramatically. Our attention turns from heaven to earth, from the praise and worship of God to His wrath and judgment upon mankind. All creation stands in awe as Christ opens the seven-sealed scroll.

In preparation for this lesson, read Revelation 6:1–8.

YOU ARE HERE

Do you recall when you first considered the idea of God's judgment? For some of us, judgment may have been presented as the final, fiery destination for sinners. For others, judgment may be interpreted as the "bad things" that happen to us here on earth because of our sin—calamity, illness, inconveniences—the proverbial lightning bolts from heaven! Many Christians first learned about the final judgments of God from Sunday-school charts or in books about the end times, understanding them as future events directed at the sinful world but detached from our present concerns—situations we don't need to worry about or prepare for.

Most people would prefer to ignore the idea of a judging God or even completely deny that God would judge anybody for anything. After all, isn't God a loving God? How can judgment and love coexist? With all of these confusing images and interpretations as well as our own natural human fear of judgment, it's no wonder that we find the end times and related topics to be controversial and even disturbing.

Describe your initial reaction to the word *judgment*. Is it positive or negative?

_____

_____

_____

Before you were a believer, how did you understand God's judgment?

_____

_____

_____

How has your understanding changed as you learned more about God's character and His actions throughout history?

_____

_____

_____

 DISCOVERING THE WAY

In the first leg of John's heavenly journey, he visited the glorious throne room of God (Revelation 4–5), where he saw the almighty God holding a seven-sealed scroll—a title deed of absolute ownership over the world. Only one Person in heaven and earth was found worthy to take the scroll, open its seals, and begin the step-by-step process of snatching control of the world from evil, ultimately extinguishing sin and death: Jesus Christ.

However, the process of establishing His kingdom on earth will involve a period of unparalleled judgment followed by indescribable glory. This process of judgment requires careful study, as it can be difficult to understand or even disturbing to comprehend.

GETTING THE BIG PICTURE OF FUTURE JUDGMENTS

Three symbols represent three different series of future judgments in the book of Revelation: seven seals, seven trumpets, and seven bowls. Each series describes unique events of the coming Tribulation, and the effects of the judgments overlap so that they intensify toward the end and culminate at the return of Christ.

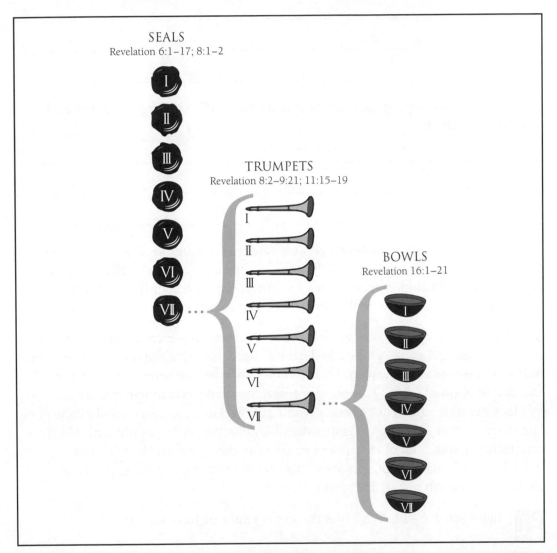

SEALS
Revelation 6:1–17; 8:1–2

TRUMPETS
Revelation 8:2–9:21; 11:15–19

BOWLS
Revelation 16:1–21

Although an awareness of this structure may seem irrelevant, we can discover a few important truths through an understanding of the big picture.

First, *the warning itself demonstrates God's grace*. The fact that God has revealed the seriousness and severity of these judgments so far in advance of their coming demonstrates grace in allowing us to turn to Christ before they begin.

 Read 2 Peter 3:3–9. God promised that Christ would return in judgment. How do many unbelievers respond to this warning?

_____

_____

_____

What are God's purposes in warning us about His coming judgment and delaying its advent?

_____

_____

_____

Second, *each series of judgments grows in severity*. Although God would be completely justified in choosing to end the world in one quick flash, by His mercy He has determined to allow opportunities for repentance even after the judgments begin. God desires not only to judge the wicked but also to bring sinners to repentance.

Third, *God's judgments are completely under His control*—even when they are carried out by natural events and wicked people. Recognize that the initial action of each judgment takes place in heaven. Then and only then are the actors on earth commanded or allowed to act. This process guarantees that God's judgments are tempered by His grace and remain in complete harmony with His dual purposes of establishing His kingdom and ushering in righteousness. Unlike the actions of humans, God's actions never spiral out of His control or do more damage than He deliberately intends. His ultimate purpose is always to demonstrate His matchless power and glory, even through justice and wrath (Romans 9:22).

 Read Job 1:6–12. Who was the *direct* cause of Job's suffering?

_____

_____

Who had the *ultimate* authority over Job's suffering?

_____

_____

Does this truth comfort you or trouble you in regard to your own experiences of suffering? How does this principle relate to the future judgments recorded in Revelation?

_____

_____

_____

DIGGING DEEPER
Does God Cause *Judgment or* Allow *Judgment?*

We often try to shy away from the concept of an angry, wrathful, or judging God, choosing instead to imagine a loving, gracious, and tolerant God. When we become acquainted with God's judgments in the book of Revelation, however, we see a harmonious balance between His justice and grace, His mercy and wrath.

God is just in punishing evil; evil deserves to be judged. But God, in His abundant grace, tempers His wrath and demonstrates mercy. For example, in Mark 13:20, Jesus taught that God would shorten the days of the Tribulation; otherwise, His judgments would be so severe that everyone in the world would perish. However, in spite of His mercy, the Tribulation will include His most severe judgments of all time.

Most of the judgments in Revelation come through the work of evil agents. God *allows* evil in the world, but He is not the author of evil. One theologian writes,

> Specifically, it will not do to accuse God of evil intentions or malevolent acts. He is sovereign, but not blameworthy, for He is righteous in all His deeds (Ps. 11:7; Dan. 9:14). He oversees all things in accord with His will, but He is not the source, the cause, or the author of sin." [1]

Continued on next page

Continued from previous page

As you read through the book of Revelation, it may appear that the world has spun out of control *because* of terrible evil and severe judgments. Remember that God is always sovereign. And just as God is in control of all extreme, cataclysmic events, He's in control of the trials and tribulations in our lives (Psalm 115:3; 135:5–6).

UNDERSTANDING THE FIRST FOUR SEAL JUDGMENTS
(REVELATION 6:1–8)

Now that we've studied the general order and relevance of the three series of judgments, let's begin our study with the first four seal judgments in Revelation 6:1–2, better known as the "Four Horsemen of the Apocalypse."

Read Revelation 6:1–8 again. In the following chart, make observations about what John saw and heard, then note the similarities and differences between the four horsemen. Be as detailed as possible.

	First Seal 6:1–2	Second Seal 6:3–4	Third Seal 6:5–6	Fourth Seal 6:7–8
Observations	white horse bow / crown conquerer bent on conquest no arrows	fiery red one take peace away make people kil each other	black horse pair of scales 2 lbs wheat for days wages 6 lbs barley for days wages do not damage oil & wine	pale horse death 1/4 earth kill) by sword, famine, plague wild beast
Similarities				
Differences	Saves but fake peace	torment	living on basic	1/4 population killed

What was "given" or "granted" to each of the riders? Who do you think gave them these things or abilities?

_____

_____

_____

The images of the four horsemen are heavy with symbolism, and commentators have long debated the specific meaning of each one. However, the big picture is easily apparent long before we begin to look into the details: severe judgment is coming, but God has everything under control. Beyond this truth, some familiarity with the possible meanings of these symbols will help us to understand how God will work out His plan for the future.

The rider on the white horse represents bloodless conquest—false peace and security. He carries a bow without arrows. The type of crown on his head is the *stephanos*, a word which does not suggest regal authority but a victor's crown.[2] The Great Tribulation will begin with a deceptive peace, and it will be accompanied by a counterfeit spirituality and a false religion.

Read 1 Thessalonians 5:2–3. Summarize the general condition of the world as it is presented in these prophetic words of Paul.

On a ordinary day & season
_____

_____

How does this description relate to the conditions symbolized by the rider on the white horse in Revelation 6:1–2?

deceptive peace
_____

_____

_____

Immediately after the ride of the white horse promising peace and security, the rider on the red horse breaks the promise. The red color symbolizes the fire and blood of war. Rather than an arrowless bow symbolizing the mere threat of conflict from a distance, this dreaded rider carries a sword. And this sword is not the *rhomphaia* of order and justice that comes from the mouth of Christ (Revelation 1:16; 2:12, 16), but the *machaira* of assassinations, insurrection, and warfare.[3]

After the beckoning of the third living creature, John watches a black horse leap forth. As this symbol of the famine and poverty that results from warfare comes into view, desolation and despair wrap their tentacles around the globe. The measuring scales and the voice shouting out prices indicate that this period of time will be characterized by inflation and starvation. One commentator writes:

> The prices listed here are about eight to sixteen times the average prices in the Roman Empire at the time. . . . Therefore, those suffering from the famine will only be able to buy limited food quantities for their family, and there will be nothing left over to provide for any of the other necessities of life such as "wine and oil."[4]

With the opening of the fourth seal, the fourth horse charges into John's view. The Greek word describing its color is *chlōros*, a "yellowish green,"[5] the sickly color of illness and death. In this macabre, terrifying scene, John saw the grim reaper and the gravedigger moving across the face of the earth. Death steals the body while Hades consumes the soul. These two symbols represent the massive number of deaths that will follow in the wake of the first three horsemen. One-quarter of the world's population will be lost in their rampage.

As a review, compare the symbolic portrayals in Revelation 6:1–8 with the literal prophecies of Matthew 24:4–9, noting the terms Christ uses to describe these same events. Then, choose a name for each rider in Revelation 6, using your own words.

Matthew	Revelation	Observations	Name
24:4–5	6:1–2	False messiah	Retoric ;false messiah
24:6–7	6:3–4	wars, nation against nation famines, earth quakes	Futile wars
24:7–8	6:5–6	beginning stages famine	Hungry world
24:9	6:7–8	you will be persecuted & put to death; hated by all nations because of me.	Grim Reaper

As we try to come to terms with the severity of these judgments, we must remember that all of the wars, pestilence, death, and destruction throughout history pale in comparison to this outpouring of God's wrath. And we should also keep in mind that these first four seals of judgment are "merely the beginning of birth pangs" (Matthew 24:8). The worst is yet to come.

Describe your initial response to John's description of the first series of judgments. How do they make you feel about God, humanity, the world, and the future?

It's a lot like the Israel during the reign of bad kings. Eyes seeing but not looking, ears hearing but not comprehend

How do they make you feel about the present?

Prepare with seriousness

What do you find most difficult to accept about these judgments? Why do you feel this way?

Sad the thing is that everything seems to head that way. Ever slowly we are at pt of no return.

 STARTING YOUR JOURNEY
Coming to terms with God's judgment is difficult, especially in our world today. We want to emphasize the love, grace, and mercy of God and ignore the anger, wrath, and judgment of God. Those who claim to be "spiritual" rather than "religious" seek a god who gushes with affirmation, encourages freedom of self-expression, and winks at our daily mistakes. That type of god, created in our own image, is nothing like the God of the Bible, as we can clearly see in the book of Revelation.

How does a believer in Jesus Christ come to terms with God's judgment? First, *we give Him praise for delivering us from it*. He promised to deliver believers from the coming wrath, so we must take His prophecies of future judgments seriously, but we should not fear them.

The following passages promise believers that they will be delivered from the coming wrath. Read all of them, and then select two or three to memorize, thanking God that He will deliver us from wrath through Jesus Christ.

Romans 5:9

1 Thessalonians 1:10

1 Thessalonians 5:9

Second, *believers must urge others to trust Christ, so that they, too, will escape the coming wrath*. If you knew a disaster was about to strike, you would warn people to stay away. In the same manner, Christians should warn unbelievers of the coming judgment so they can avoid it.

Whom do you need to begin praying for in regard to their eternal salvation? Besides prayer, what else can you do to share Christ with these people?

_____

_____

_____

How should unbelievers respond to the warning of God's judgments? As harsh as it may sound in today's inclusive culture, unbelievers have no hope apart from Christ. As Hebrews 10:31 says, "It is a terrifying thing to fall into the hands of the living God." However, we must take heart. The judgments have not yet begun. The four horsemen have not yet begun their terrible ride of destruction. We still have time to respond.

If you are unsure about your own relationship with God, or if you want to review how to share the good news about Jesus Christ with others, read "How to Begin a Relationship with God" at the end of this book.

 In your own words, list at least three purposes for God's future judgments.

_____

_____

_____

Take a few minutes to pause and pray, thanking and praising God for who He is and what He will do in the future, and confessing any questions or concerns you have about judgment in general or the descriptions of the seal judgments in particular.

_____

_____

_____

❖

In this lesson we learned that God's judgments are not pointless. Each one has a definite purpose—He seeks to bring sinners to repentance, judge the wicked, wrest control of the world away from Satan, establish His kingdom, usher in righteousness, and demonstrate His own power and glory. In response to His justice and wrath, believers must be moved to worship God with humility and awe.

REVELATION

"I am the Alpha . . ." (1:8) . . . "and the Omega" (22:13)

	"The things which you have seen . . ." Personal and biographical	"The things which are . . ." Christ's letters to the seven churches	"The things which will take place . . ." (Revelation 1:19) Christ as Judge (chaps. 4–5) The Tribulation (chaps. 6–18) The Coming of Christ (chap. 19) The Millennium (chap. 20) The Eternal State (chaps. 21–22)
	CHAPTER 1	*CHAPTERS 2–3*	*CHAPTERS 4–22*
Scope	History: looking back		Prophecy: looking ahead
Style	Dialogue		Observations and questions
Scene	On earth		Shifts between earth and heaven
Main Theme	Christ's future triumph over the forces of evil and His re-creation of the world for the redeemed		
Key Verses	1:7, 19; 22:12–13		

LESSON TWO

MORE SEALS BROKEN...
MORE LIVES SHAKEN AND TAKEN

Revelation 6:9–17

THE HEART OF THE MATTER

Chaos, misery, sorrow, and grief will sweep across the earth as God
unleashes His future judgments. Yet those dreaded events will occur in
God's timing as set forth in the book of Revelation. Nothing will be able
to restrain the coming judgments or diminish their impact. As John watches Christ
breaking the fifth and sixth seals of the seven-sealed scroll, we begin to witness the
future fate of both believers and unbelievers during the Tribulation.

In preparation for this lesson, read Revelation 6:9–17.

YOU ARE HERE

Our morning rituals are often the same, day-in and day-out. Wake up.
Wash and dress. Eat breakfast. Say goodbye to our spouses and children.
Head off to another day of work. Like a religious rite, we expect our
routine to be the same every single day. But each one of us has experienced an unexpected disruption—a flat tire, a sick child, a phone call out of the blue relaying tragic
news. Situations like these interrupt our routine with unwelcome stress—even severe
trials. Occasionally these events can upset a person's entire life.

For most, God's judgment during the end times will be unexpected and unwel-
come, disrupting life's routine with more than just minor irritation. The Great
Tribulation of Matthew 24:21 will affect more than just one family, city, or nation.
God's judgment will affect the whole world (Luke 17:26–30; 1 Thessalonians 5:1–3;
Revelation 3:10).

How would you respond if an unbeliever told you, "If the prophecies described in Revelation start to come true, *then* I'll believe in Jesus"?

_____

_____

_____

Suppose a person becomes a believer during the Tribulation described in Revelation. What do you think the life of a believer will be like during that time?

_____

_____

_____

What will the life of an unbeliever be like during the Tribulation?

_____

_____

_____

How do you know?

_____

_____

_____

DISCOVERING THE WAY

We all want to know where we're going. We buy maps to keep from getting lost, seek advice to avoid making bad decisions, and pray for the Lord's guidance when we're confused about His will. In fact, in most cases we're much more interested in the future than the past. Teach a class on history, and you'll be lucky if a handful of people show up; but teach a class on prophecy, and you'd better order extra chairs!

The disciples of Jesus felt the same way. As they walked with Jesus on the Mount of Olives, several disciples asked questions about the future — "Tell us, when will these things happen, and what will be the sign of Your coming, and of the end of the age?" (Matthew 24:3). After Christ's resurrection, the disciples' curiosity about the coming kingdom was as keen as ever. At the end of forty days with the risen Lord, they asked, "Lord, is it at this time You are restoring the kingdom to Israel?" (Acts 1:6).

 If you were asked, how would you answer the following questions?

"When will the events of the end times begin to occur?"

_____

_____

_____

"What signs will indicate that the end times have begun?"

_____

_____

_____

REVIEW OF THE FIRST FOUR SEALS (REVELATION 6:1–8)

Christ's answer to the "when question" was always the same: no one can know the timing of these events. Everything will come to pass according to the Father's master plan (Acts 1:7; 1 Thessalonians 5:5–6). However, Christ does tell the disciples — and us — what the end times will look like. We studied some of these events in the previous lesson, and we will continue to explore the next two seals in this lesson.

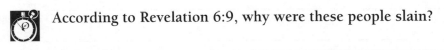 Without consulting the Bible or your answers to the questions in the previous lesson, list the four events symbolized by the four horsemen in Revelation 6 and described by Christ in Matthew 24. You may want to use the key words you came up with in the last lesson to help you remember.

1. _____

2. _____

3. _____

4. _____

Let's summarize for a moment. When the seven-year Tribulation begins, a political/religious leader will rise to prominence on the world stage, accompanied by signs, wonders, and the ability to usher in a false peace and security. Much of the world will follow him. However, his false peace will fall to pieces when war breaks out, followed by famine, disease, and a shattered world economy. These rumblings will intensify, causing the death of one in four people worldwide. And the worst is yet to come.

THE FIFTH SEAL: MARTYRDOM (REVELATION 6:9–11)

After watching the four horsemen begin their gallop across the darkening landscape, the apostle John witnessed the Lamb breaking the fifth seal, marking the next event of the Great Tribulation.

According to Revelation 6:9, why were these people slain?

_____

_____

_____

What did they cry out for in 6:10?

_____

_____

_____

What was God's response in 6:11?

_____

_____

_____

God set a limit on the number of martyrs He would allow during the Tribulation. Does this truth trouble you or comfort you? Why?

_____

_____

_____

Read Revelation 12:17; 13:7, 15; 14:12–13, and describe what life will be like during the Tribulation for those who choose to believe at that time.

_____

_____

_____

What is the ultimate destiny of these martyrs according to Revelation 20:4?

_____

_____

_____

DOORWAY TO HISTORY
White Robes

In Revelation 7:14, the martyrs are given "white robes." The Greek term for these robes is *stolō*, which refers to a "long, flowing robe."[1] These white robes signified a person's high social or religious status (Mark 12:38; Luke 15:22), and they were also worn by angels to indicate their heavenly brilliance. The saints who were martyred during the Great Tribulation wear these *stolō* (Revelation 7:9, 13, 14), and earlier in Revelation the image of wearing white signifies a future reward for worthiness (3:3–4; 4:4; 6:11).

White robes commonly symbolized rewards for the righteous in the future kingdom, as seen by a reference to the glorious destiny of the saints made in the Dead Sea Scrolls: "It shall be healing, great peace in a long life, and fruitfulness, together with every everlasting blessing and eternal joy in life without end, a crown of glory and a garment of majesty in unending light."[2] In the ancient world, white, flowing robes would have signified a beautiful reward for lives lived in jeopardy and sacrificed for the sake of Jesus Christ.

The fifth seal provides us with some understanding of the fate of believers during the Tribulation. The church, now with God, having been rescued from wrath before the beginning of the Tribulation, will already have received their new, glorified bodies and rewards for their faithfulness (Revelation 3:10).[3] They will have true, eternal peace and security. However, those who come to faith in Christ *during* the seven-year Tribulation period will face the greatest persecution and martyrdom the world has ever known (Matthew 24:21). Yet these martyrs who suffer at the hands of the Antichrist (Revelation 13) will ultimately be vindicated when God pours out His wrath over the earth.

Throughout the history of the church, believers have experienced persecution and martyrdom. How do you think John's glimpse of the martyrs' fate would have comforted the original readers of Revelation as they endured their own trials and tribulations?

_____

_____

_____

Does this image comfort you? Why, or why not?

_____

_____

_____

THE SIXTH SEAL: THE DAY OF WRATH (REVELATION 6:12–17)

The Great Tribulation will be a time of terrible martyrdom . . . but vengeance will follow. Answering the call of the Tribulation martyrs who cried out for vindication, the sixth seal reveals the horror of unbelievers who must face the full wrath of God and His appointed Judge, Jesus Christ.

 In your own words, list the phenomena described in Revelation 6:12–14. What kinds of responses were these images intended to elicit from the readers of Revelation?

_____

_____

_____

 According to Revelation 6:15, who responds to these natural disasters?

_____

_____

Are any classes of people missing from this list?

_____

_____

What does this list reveal about the extent of the judgments during the coming Tribulation?

_____

_____

_____

Are those who become believers during the Tribulation members of this group as well? Why, or why not?

_____

_____

_____

John used the most descriptive terms he could possibly use to describe the severity of these upheavals of heaven and earth. We can easily imagine the types of geological events that might cause such phenomena. A great earthquake shakes the entire globe, and volcanic eruptions spew ash and gases into the atmosphere, veiling the sun like a rough, burlap cloth. Putrid air distorts the color of the moon, and the heavens rain down meteors. Whatever the ultimate fulfillment of these images, we can agree with one commentator who writes, "The scene . . . is one of catastrophe and distress for the inhabitants of the earth."[4]

Following these events, John was exposed to a frightful scene: the complete and utter panic of the entire population of the world. Recent terrorist attacks and natural disasters have given us a brief glimpse of widespread fear and anxiety like this. The same emotions and reactions exist in John's vision, though they are greatly intensified by the addition of pervasive hopelessness.

The Seven Seals		
First Seal	False Peace and Security	Revelation 6:1–2
Second Seal	Warfare and Bloodshed	Revelation 6:3–4
Third Seal	Famine and Poverty	Revelation 6:5–6
Fourth Seal	Death and Natural Disasters	Revelation 6:7–8
Fifth Seal	Martyrdom of Believers	Revelation 6:9–11
Sixth Seal	Worldwide Catastrophes	Revelation 6:12–17
Seventh Seal	Seven Trumpets	Revelation 8:1–2

Recall a recent event of disaster or tragedy. How did those closest to the event respond? Describe their emotions, attitudes, and actions. How do their responses compare with the reactions described in Revelation 6:15–17?

_____

_____

_____

_____

_____

STARTING YOUR JOURNEY
The late Bible teacher, John Walvoord, challenged believers regarding our response to Revelation 6:

> The contents of chapter 6 should put to rest the false teachings that God, being a God of love, could not judge a wicked world. It also raises the important question contained in the closing words of verse 17: **Who can stand?** Only those who have availed themselves of the grace of God before the time of judgment will be able to stand when God deals with the earth in this final period of great distress.[5]

Every single one of us is called to answer the crucial question of Revelation 6:17, "Who is able to stand?" Because of sin, humans have hidden from the presence of God ever since the day Adam and Eve rebelled in the garden of Eden (Genesis 3:9–10). However, when the period of God's wrath begins, the guilty will not be able to hide from the judgments of God. All people of the world—small or great, rich or poor—will suddenly lose all of their peace and security. The very foundations of their lives will be shaken as food vanishes, money becomes worthless, and possessions become irrelevant. Only rank desperation for physical survival will remain. In a time of such desolation, who will be "able to stand?"

Take a moment to examine your life in light of this lesson. If the events of Revelation were to begin today, would you be prepared? Why, or why not?

_____

_____

_____

Whether or not you are "able to stand" against the trials and temptations of this world depends on who stands with you. If you are unsure about where you stand in relationship to Jesus Christ, read "How to Begin a Relationship with God" at the end of this book. What must you do to be "able to stand" in an eternal sense?

_____

_____

_____

Those who become believers during the Great Tribulation will receive the strength they will need to endure extreme persecution and martyrdom. Though God promises to save those who already believe from that coming period of wrath (1 Thessalonians 1:10; 5:9), He will provide us with the same spiritual strength as we endure our own present trials and struggles against sin, Satan, and the world.

Read the following passages, and summarize the practical steps we should take to become "able to stand" through our own personal struggles.

Ephesians 6:10–18

_____

_____

_____

Jude 24–25

_____

_____

_____

What actions will you take to become "able to stand" in the midst of the challenges of this present world?

_____

_____

_____

Revelation dispels the myth that the triune God winks at sin or is too mild and loving to actually punish wickedness. The theme of God executing vengeance on behalf of His people is also found elsewhere in the New Testament.

Observe what the following passages teach concerning God's vengeance and the appropriate response of believers.

Romans 12:19–21

_____

_____

2 Thessalonians 1:6–10

_____

_____

Hebrews 10:30–31

_____

_____

In light of these passages, how should you respond to the persecution and affliction in your life?

_____

_____

_____

⁓❧⁓

The dreaded events of the Tribulation will impact all people living during that time — those who choose to believe and those who harden their hearts in unbelief. Yet in His grace, God will provide strength to those Tribulation saints who suffer persecution and martyrdom, comfort and reward to those who lose everything for the sake of Christ, and ultimately vengeance to those servants of Satan who are guilty of blood. In our present trials and tribulations, we can have confidence in the same God who will strengthen and comfort believers in the end times. Are you relying on His strength today?

AN INTERLUDE: EARTHLY RESTRAINT AND HEAVENLY WORSHIP

Revelation 7:1–17

THE HEART OF THE MATTER

By the end of the judgment of the sixth seal described in Revelation 6, many frightened people hid themselves in caves and among rocks. In the shock of the day of God's wrath, they asked, "Who is able to stand?" (Revelation 6:17). The Lord brought the seal judgments to a pause, almost as if He wished to answer that question. In that moment, John saw heavenly angels providing supernatural protection for a certain number of God's people. His unshakeable security stands in sharp contrast to the panic of the pagan world. In Revelation 7 we see not one but *two* distinct groups of the redeemed—144,000 protected, converted Jews on earth and an innumerable multitude of martyred, white-robed saints in heaven.

In preparation for this lesson, read Revelation 7:1–17.

YOU ARE HERE

An old Greek proverb says, "You'll break a bow if you always keep it bent." In other words, everybody needs a break from time to time. Constant work, day in and day out, without a time of reprieve and rest, will result in the breaking of a spirit, a body, and a life. People under unrelenting stress and strain will eventually crack. The principle of rest is woven into the week of God's creation (Genesis 1) and remains a fundamental principle in the lives of humans today. Sadly, most people do not fully appreciate this need, and they miss the spiritual benefits that come from rest.

Recall a time when you were able to take a long-overdue vacation from a hectic schedule, stressful work, or even intense agony and pain. How did you feel during that rest? Were you able to truly relax? Why, or why not?

_____

_____

_____

What was the result of your rest? Was the source of your stress easier to bear? In what way?

_____

_____

_____

 DISCOVERING THE WAY

After unleashing a traumatic series of visions (Revelation 6), the Lord knew John was ready for a break. Between the sixth and seventh seal judgments of Revelation 7, John was provided a much-needed interlude—one that we will appreciate as we continue our study together. At the end of chapter 6, we heard nothing but screaming from the mountains: "Who is able to stand?" The next vision provides an answer to that question.

 Read Revelation 6:16–17. Do you think these people believed that anyone would be able to stand in the midst of God's wrath? Why, or why not?

_____

_____

_____

Supernatural Protection for Israel (Revelation 7:1–8)

As the hoofbeats of the four horsemen echoed into the distance and the cacophony of geological and cosmic upheavals stilled, God turned John's attention to the center of the earthly drama: the land of Israel. Throughout its history the people of Israel have been conquered, delivered, devastated, exiled, and restored over and over again as military threats bombarded them from every side. Yet at the beginning of the Tribulation, just as the land of Israel—as well as the rest of the earth—is about to endure the most devastating war in all of history, God intervenes and reminds John (and us) that He will keep His promises to Israel.

At the opening of the vision in Revelation 7, God sent four angels to hold back "the four winds of the earth"—a symbol for delaying the coming judgments that would affect the earth and sea (Revelation 7:1–2). Another angel holding "the seal of the living God" cried out to the four angels, "Do not harm the earth or the sea or the trees until we have sealed the bond-servants of our God on their foreheads" (Revelation 7:3). A detailed roster of these Hebrews follows in Revelation 7:4–8.

Read Revelation 7:1–4. Who was sealed? How are they described?

_____

_____

_____

If we compare this list of the twelve tribes with any other lists in the Old Testament, we may note a few differences.[1] Perhaps if John himself were to have composed the list, he would have followed one of the patterns found in the Old Testament. However, according to Revelation 7:4, John simply wrote down what he heard without asking any questions. Later, as he reviewed the names of the twelve tribes, he may have even scratched his head. *The list includes Levi? It leaves out Dan? It replaces Ephraim with Joseph?* Though we may not be able to fully explain why these particular tribes were selected to make up the 144,000, we can trust that God had His reasons.[2]

These 144,000 Jews will serve as faithful, pure, and diligent witnesses for Christ during the darkest period of the earth's history, and God will use them in the midst of evil as a force for good. God's plan for Israel was always for the people to serve as the light of truth for the Gentile nations. In the Tribulation they will serve as Christ's bond servants who finally fulfill this mission. This believing remnant from ethnic

Israel will not only be sealed for power and protection, but they will also survive the Tribulation period and compose the nation of Israel restored to the land during the coming millennial kingdom.

 Based on the following passages, what else is true of the 144,000 who are sealed at the beginning of the Tribulation?

Revelation 9:3–4

_____

_____

_____

Revelation 14:1–5

_____

_____

_____

DIGGING DEEPER
Future for Israel

Many Christians today believe that God's plan for ethnic Israel has come to an end; that the promises of a glorious nation and blessing in the land have been abolished—or perhaps fulfilled in a spiritual sense in the church. Some theologians even propose that Israel has been replaced by the church—utterly rejected, divorced, and without a future in God's plan.

However, the New Testament tells us that God's plan is not to reinterpret the promises for ethnic Israel but to bring about the fulfillment of those promises through Jesus Christ. Although most of ethnic Israel has been in a state of unbelief since the time of Jesus, God will one day bring a remnant to faith in Christ and restore them in the land promised to their forefathers (Genesis 13:15). Jesus Himself promised the apostles, "In the regeneration when the Son of Man will sit on His glorious throne, you also shall sit upon twelve thrones, judging the twelve tribes of Israel" (Matthew 19:28). Before Christ's ascension, the disciples eagerly inquired about the timing of that earthly kingdom when they asked, "Lord, is it at this time You are restoring the kingdom to Israel?" (Acts 1:6). Jesus did not reject their literal interpretation, but instead He told them that they would not know the timing of the restoration (Acts 1:7–8).

Years later, Paul addressed the problem of the present unbelief of most Jews by declaring that this rebellion would one day be reversed: "A partial hardening has happened to Israel until the fullness of the Gentiles has come in; and so all Israel will be saved" (Romans 11:25–26). In other words, when God has accomplished His purposes through the church, He will again turn His attention to the nation of Israel and bring them to faith in Christ. We can see the beginning of this future for Israel with the sealing of the 144,000 in Revelation 7:1–8.

Why is the restoration of Israel so important? God's very reputation as a promise-keeper is on the line. Paul said, "For the gifts and the calling of God are irrevocable" (Romans 11:29). If we cannot trust God to keep His promises to Israel (Jeremiah 31:35–37), then we cannot trust Him to keep His promises to us (Romans 8:35–39). One commentator addresses this issue in his discussion of Revelation 7:1–8, "The most important fact taught here is that God continues to watch over Israel even in the time of Israel's great distress."[3] In the same way, God watches over believers today.

Read Jeremiah 31. In this passage, God declared the advent of the new covenant — made possible by the death of Christ and to be fulfilled by Him (Luke 22:20; 2 Corinthians 3:6). Answer the following questions based on Jeremiah's prophecy.

Who will take part in the new covenant (31:31–32)?

_____

List at least four benefits of the new covenant (31:33–34).

_____

_____

_____

According to Jeremiah 31:35–37, what would have to happen for God to abandon Israel? Is this possible or likely? Then what has God promised here?

_____

_____

_____

What other blessings are associated with the fulfillment of the new covenant (31:38–40)?

_____

_____

_____

Have these prophecies been fulfilled?

_____

BLISSFUL PRAISE FROM NUMEROUS NATIONS
(REVELATION 7:9–17)

One of the most frequently asked questions in regard to the Tribulation is whether or not anyone will come to saving faith in Jesus Christ during that difficult time. We have already observed that 144,000 people from various tribes of ethnic Israel will be set apart for the Lord. But they will not be alone! Perhaps through the stellar testimonies of the 144,000, God will call to Himself a countless number of believers in Jesus "from every nation and all tribes and peoples and tongues" (Revelation 7:9). However, in contrast to the protected number of Hebrew believers in 7:1–8, these Gentile believers will suffer persecution and martyrdom. In fact, when John's vision of the great multitude opened, these believers were already pictured in heaven, having suffered physical death at the hands of God's enemies.

How does the description of the great multitude in Revelation 7:9–10 differ from that of the 144,000 in 7:3–4?

_____

_____

_____

Where did this great multitude come from (7:13–14)?

_____

What is their function in heaven (7:15–17)?

_____

_____

_____

Based on Revelation 7:16–17, what do you think these martyrs experienced during the Tribulation? Why will they need comfort?

_____

_____

_____

Those who come to believe during the Great Tribulation will be in one of two groups. The first group of believers will be the remnant of physical Israel sealed for protection and called to testify concerning Christ (Revelation 7:1–8). The second group of believers will be composed of the masses of Gentiles who believe in Christ and suffer persecution and martyrdom for their faith. These martyrs will come out of the Great Tribulation through death, but their suffering will instantly give way to victorious worship as they join the heavenly chorus in praise to "our God who sits on the throne, and to the Lamb" (Revelation 7:10).

STARTING YOUR JOURNEY

In the midst of the increasingly intense judgments of Revelation 6 and following, God granted John an interlude of mercy in Revelation 7. Here we witness the salvation of people from every tribe and also catch a glimpse of the final fulfillment of God's age-old promises to the nation of Israel. The characters are in place, the stage is set, and the action is ready to continue in Revelation 8. However, before we return to the earthly drama in the next lesson, let's pause for a few practical principles for reflection and response.

First, *the interlude in Revelation 7 reaffirms Christ's central position.* The chaos of the fallen world should drive us to find peace and rest in Jesus Christ. He is the Lamb who is also our Shepherd, and He will provide comfort and provision in all our times of need (Revelation 7:16–17). And as we return to Christ as the center of our lives, we also reaffirm the priority of worship—praising God for who He is and what He has done for us (Revelation 7:10–12).

Besides your relationship with Jesus Christ, list your other top four priorities in life.

1. *My relationship with Christ*

2. _____

3. _____

4. _____

5. _____

Of these five priorities, which do you feel is central in your life?

_____

As you reflect on your daily schedule, which of these priorities takes up most of your time, energy, and finances?

_____

Are you pleased with this evaluation? Why, or why not? Would the Lord be pleased?

_____

_____

_____

Second, *the interlude in Revelation 7 reminds us of what is important.* As humans, we are prone to lose sight of the real priorities in life, especially during times of trials and temptations. Most circumstances in this world are temporary, but the spiritual realities that seem so shadowy and distant now will one day be revealed as eternal. Deliberately reflecting on what's really important will help us remain calm and focused even in the midst of struggles.

Has the daily grind forced you to the ground? Do you need an interlude from the daily stress of life? Then consider taking a family vacation or a weekend getaway. However, don't just use this time to relax and play. Instead, reflect and pray. Think through your priorities, Christ's place in your life, and your response to His promises and provision. In the space below, note your ideas for such a retreat, and then take steps to make it a reality.

_____

_____

_____

Third, *the interlude in Revelation 7 reminds us why life is worthwhile.* When we have a backstage pass to see the heavenly reality behind the earthly drama, we begin to make sense out of suffering, understand loss, and handle disappointments. Such interludes provide a fresh, new start and give us the energy we need to continue on. Revelation 7 provides an interlude in God's judgments to remember His mercy—specifically the mercy He shows to Israel, His ancient people of promise. This passage should remind us that God will keep *all* of His promises—and that includes the promises He has given to us.

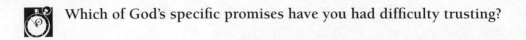 **Which of God's specific promises have you had difficulty trusting?**

_____

_____

_____

    Write a prayer confessing your faith in Him and declaring your trust in His promises. Be specific.

_____

_____

_____

_____

_____

_____

Revelation 7 reminds us that God keeps His promises to His people through the person of Jesus Christ. However, we can often lose sight both of the promises and the Promise-Keeper in the midst of the daily turmoil of life. Only during interludes of reflection are we able to evaluate our priorities and passions in light of the central position of Jesus Christ. In turn, these interludes will equip us to step out into the fray with a new sense of purpose as we place our trust in Him.

FIRST BLASTS OF THE TRUMPET PLAGUES

Revelation 8:1–13

THE HEART OF THE MATTER

Through the visions of Revelation 8, we leave the quiet interlude in Revelation 7 that announced the salvation of Jews and Gentiles during the Tribulation, and we return to the divine judgments that will assault the earth. With the breaking of the seventh seal, the series of seven trumpet blasts begins, causing even greater devastation and chaos than the previous judgments. As these blasts intensify, we are reminded that God has a purpose for His judgments—to call unbelievers to repentance and to announce to believers that the day of His vengeance has come.

In preparation for this lesson, read Revelation 8:1–13.

YOU ARE HERE

Reflecting on the problem of pain and suffering in our fallen world, Christian apologist C. S. Lewis wrote the following:

Anyone who has watched gluttons shoveling down the most exquisite foods as if they did not know what they were eating, will admit that we can ignore even pleasure. But pain insists upon being attended to. God whispers to us in our pleasures, speaks in our conscience, but shouts in our pains: it is His megaphone to rouse a deaf world.[1]

In your experience, does pain and suffering in the world tend to draw people to God or turn them away from Him? Explain your answer.

_____

_____

_____

Why will two people who experience the same natural disaster or personal tragedy respond differently? What factors may determine how they will react to God in difficult situations?

_____

_____

_____

 According to Romans 3:9–12, what is the natural condition of every person in relation to God? Be specific, using words from the passage itself.

_____

_____

_____

How does our condition affect our response to God's revelation?

_____

_____

_____

Read the previous quote by C. S. Lewis once more. If God wanted to use pain to get the attention of the whole world, how effective do you think it would be? Give specific reasons for your answer.

_____

_____

_____

Read Matthew 12:38–40 and 13:13–17. What did the skeptics ask of Jesus? How did they respond to Him?

_____

_____

_____

What does this reveal about humanity's natural response to works of God intended to demonstrate His power?

_____

_____

_____

DISCOVERING THE WAY

Human beings are a stubborn lot! When you combine our strong wills, spiritual blindness, rebellious spirits, and selfish ambitions, it's a miracle that any of us turn from ourselves to God for salvation (Matthew 19:25–26; John 6:44). In the process of leading people to repentance, God uses a variety of means, and when He wants to capture the attention of the entire world, He uses an intensifying series of judgments. In fact, we could say that a major purpose of God's judgments in Revelation is to seize the world's attention when it refuses to listen.

A Brief Calm before the Storm (Revelation 8:1–4)

After John witnessed Christ opening the first six seals of the seven-sealed scroll (Revelation 5–6), he caught a backstage glimpse of the multitude of Jews and Gentiles who would be saved during the Tribulation (Revelation 7). Following this brief intermission, the second act of God's judgments was ready to begin at the opening of the seventh seal (Revelation 8:1). To capture the world's attention, God's angels sounded a series of trumpets—unmistakable signs of His power over the earth. For some, the sound will serve as a call to faith and repentance . . . but for most, it will be a terrifying announcement of wrath.

 Read Revelation 8:1–2. Recalling the events described in Revelation 4–7, what activities suddenly ceased during this time?

_____

_____

_____

 According to the following passages, how does silence relate to judgment?

Psalm 46:10

_____

_____

_____

Psalm 76:6–9

_____

_____

_____

Isaiah 41:1–2

_____

_____

_____

Zephaniah 1:7–9

_____

_____

_____

Following the foreboding silence in heaven and the resounding warning of the angels' trumpet blasts, God deliberately responds to the prayers of the saints.

Read Revelation 8:3–4. Thinking back on the plight of the saints to this point, what do you think the content of these prayers might be? (For a hint, see Revelation 6:10.)

_____

_____

_____

We are commonly taught that God's answer to any prayer will be either "yes," "no," or "wait." In this case, we observe that unanswered prayers are sometimes stored up until God chooses to answer them in His timing. Beginning in Revelation 8:5, the time has finally come.

GETTING TO THE ROOT

Consider the definitions of these words in Revelation 8. They will help us to better understand the symbolism and significance of this passage.

Trumpet—The Greek term used here is *salpinx*, which refers to a trumpet used for a pronouncement, alarm, or call to arms. The New Testament never refers to its use as a musical instrument; it is instead a tool for military use, similar to a bugle. In Revelation, as in several Old Testament passages (Isaiah 27:13; Joel 2:1), the *salpinx* announces the day of the Lord.[2]

Censer of incense—The saucer-shaped censer was used in worship to hold burning incense, "an aromatic substance made of gums and spices."[3] In both the Old and New Testaments, the use of incense is sometimes associated with prayer (Psalm 141:2; Luke 1:10).

Wormwood—Similar to the sagebrush, wormwood is a "bitter, aromatic herb . . . with clusters of small, greenish yellow flowers" that grows in desert regions and often symbolizes the bitterness of life.[4]

BLASTS OF THE FIRST FOUR TRUMPETS (REVELATION 8:5–12)

In reference to Revelation 8, John Phillips writes, "What a potent force is prayer! The saints go into their bedrooms, close the doors, kneel down, and pray. They spread out before God their petitions, and God hears. The prayers are placed in the scales of judgment."[5] Then, in Revelation 8:5, we see God's initial response to the saints' prayer of 6:10, which precedes the systematic execution of the trumpet judgments. Phillips continues:

> Preliminary rumblings are heard, presaging the great upheavals soon to take place. Voices! Thunderings! Lightnings! Earthquakes! In its essence, this formula, sometimes called a formula for catastrophe, is repeated four times in the Apocalypse (4:5; 8:5; 11:19; 16:18). Prayer that can precipitate such things truly must be potent indeed! So the silence ends.[6]

With the conclusion of silence, the deafening blasts of the trumpets begin. In Revelation 7:3 God allowed a pause in His judgments, a delay in harming the earth, sea, and trees, until the 144,000 Israelites were sealed by His protection. When we come to the seven trumpet judgments in chapter 8, the temporary restraint of His wrath is removed.

 Complete the following chart, comparing the events that follow the first four trumpet blasts. Note the means by which each judgment is delivered, where each judgment is targeted, and the results of each judgment.

	First Trumpet (8:7)	Second Trumpet (8:8–9)	Third Trumpet (8:10–11)	Fourth Trumpet (8:12)
Means				
Target				
Results				

Which elements of these judgments are similar?

_____

_____

_____

Which elements are different?

_____

_____

_____

Recalling your answers regarding various responses to disasters in the "You Are Here" section, how do you think unbelievers will respond to the destruction described in the first four trumpet judgments?

_____

_____

_____

Read Revelation 9:20–21. How do unbelievers actually respond to these judgments? Why do you think they respond this way?

_____

_____

_____

The judgments announced by the first four trumpets are so shocking and severe that our natural tendency is to doubt their literal meaning. Of course, Revelation uses numerous symbols to communicate the future, but these symbols always point to real events. The judgments described in Revelation 8 that involve the trees, grass, seas, rivers, and atmosphere are so dreadful that no amount of government aid, volunteer work, or preparation would be able to bring about a recovery. When we're tempted to water down this language, soften its severity, or seek spiritual interpretations rather than literal ones, we must remind ourselves that Revelation describes the beginning of the end. Jesus said clearly, "For then there will be a great tribulation, such as has not occurred since the beginning of the world until now, nor ever will" (Matthew 24:21). Even the flood of Noah will pale in comparison.

Compare Pharaoh's response to Moses's words in Exodus 5:1–2 with his response in Exodus 12:31–32. How are they different?

_____

_____

Briefly skim Exodus 5 through 12. How did God bring Pharaoh to this point?

_____

_____

_____

Do you think Pharaoh's change of mind was genuine or compulsory? Why?

_____

_____

_____

How might Pharaoh's example help us understand the responses of unbelievers in Revelation?

_____

_____

_____

DIGGING DEEPER
Angels

In nearly every scene of the book of Revelation, angelic beings of various types play prominent roles in the execution of God's judgments. The scenes we watch on God's heavenly stage and in the earthly drama often stand in sharp contrast to those we see in television and movies. Hollywood's version of "angels" often reflects struggling, semi-human creatures trying to earn their wings by doing good deeds or secretly intervening in people's lives like harmless guidance counselors peddling pop psychology. In the Bible, however, we see a full cast of angelic beings that look nothing like these popular icons.

Several ranks of angelic beings appear in Scripture. Under the archangel Michael (Jude 9), the highest order is the cherubim (singular cherub, which means "one who covers"). These beings stood guard at the entrance to Eden (Genesis 3:24) and attend the presence of God (Exodus 25:18; Ezekiel 1:5–14; Revelation 4:6–8). Satan was apparently one of the cherubim before his fall (Ezekiel 28:11–19).

Besides the cherubim, Isaiah saw another high order of angels called *seraphim*, whose name means "burning ones." The seraphim are also associated with God's throne, and they may differ from the cherubim only in rank and function. These seraphim are intimately involved in God's worship (Isaiah 6:2–6), and innumerable seraphim may be the creatures that surround the throne of God in Revelation 5:11–12.

Other angels of various ranks serve God as "ministering spirits, sent out to render service for the sake of those who will inherit salvation" (Hebrews 1:14). Even though angels are among the most beautiful and powerful of all creatures, their whole existence revolves around worshiping and serving the almighty God! If these awe-inspiring beings focus their whole attention and all of their activities toward God, shouldn't we? [7]

FLYING EAGLE IN MID-HEAVEN (REVELATION 8:13)

The first four trumpet judgments, like the first four seals of Revelation 6, form a distinct cluster. They are loud, staccato blasts that seize the attention of the entire world. Following these, however, three additional judgments will come—and they will be slower, longer, and more excruciating. Before God unleashes these He makes a bold pronouncement while He has the attention of the globe. John describes the vision as follows:

> Then I looked, and I heard an eagle flying in midheaven, saying with a loud voice, "Woe, woe, woe to those who dwell on the earth, because of the remaining blasts of the trumpet of the three angels who are about to sound!" (Revelation 8:13)

The worst is yet to come.

STARTING YOUR JOURNEY
As we step away from these judgments for a moment, we cannot help but follow the example of heaven and respond in silence. No natural disaster or act of war can compare to what John has seen already—and it will only get worse. However, let's reflect on the scene described in Revelation 8 for a moment with four practical principles.

First, *God values and responds to the prayers of His people*. God may not answer your prayers instantly, but that doesn't mean He isn't listening or doesn't care. Don't stop praying!

 Have you been praying for something specific lately and feel like God isn't answering? What is it? How long have you been seeking the Lord on this matter?

_____

_____

_____

How has this made you feel about God? About yourself?

_____

_____

_____

Memorize one or more of the following passages about prayer, and be sure to recall them when you become discouraged.

Matthew 7:7–11

Ephesians 6:18

1 Thessalonians 5:17–18

1 Timothy 2:1

Second, _God uses natural disasters to communicate spiritual messages._ This truth is very difficult to accept, especially for many who have gone through the terrible disasters of recent years. God sometimes uses suffering to draw our attention to Him.

Has God ever used trials, suffering, or disasters to get your attention, correct your way, or lead you on a new path? What happened? What did you learn about God and about yourself?

_____

_____

_____

Third, _God's harsh judgments have a holy purpose._ Nobody denies that the first four trumpet judgments result in devastation, hardship, and death. Yet even in the face of God's most severe discipline, we must submit, surrender, and release our wills to Him.

Read Hebrews 12:5–11. Create three personal principles about our proper response to God's discipline.

1. _____

2. _____

3. _____

Fourth, *God won't stop until His plan is accomplished.* The sad reality of these first four trumpet judgments is that they are only the beginning. In our own lives, we can choose to heed the warnings God gives us in His Word, through fellow brothers and sisters in Christ, or in our circumstances, or we can harden our hearts. Either way, God will eventually work out His plan.

Do you sense that God has plans for your life that you are resisting? Write a prayer regarding this matter, asking the Lord to reveal any stubbornness in your heart toward His purposes and asking for His softening touch to conform your will to His in every way.

_____

_____

_____

_____

_____

In response to the prayers of the martyrs, the first group of seven trumpets blared out their announcements of wrath. Even in this time of judgment, however, God holds back the full extent of His fury in order to answer their prayers. In the same way, God will respond to our prayers. His answer may not come immediately—but He will provide it in His own sovereign timing. We must continue to stand by faithfully, awaiting His answer and submitting to His plan.

LESSON FIVE

A GLANCE BACK TO THE FUTURE

Selections from Revelation 1–8

THE HEART OF THE MATTER
Some interruptions lead to life-changing introductions. Our familiar
world sometimes comes to a screeching halt, and a whole new way of life
offers itself to us. While in exile on the island of Patmos, the apostle John
experienced a life-changing introduction to the glorious, risen Lord, Jesus Christ. He
was given a series of stunning visions that focused on Christ, the church, and the
future. In response to John's visions, we must examine our own spiritual condition in
light of the past, present, and future.

YOU ARE HERE
Many of us have read sensational books about the end times or watched
television preachers point to a current event as the fulfillment of a particular passage of biblical prophecy. The cryptic and confusing images in
the book of Revelation have been misinterpreted and twisted for centuries—and the
same continues today. If we fail to understand the big picture, we can easily misinterpret the details.

But what, exactly, is the big picture?

**If you had to decide on a *single* word to summarize the most important
message or theme of the book of Revelation, what would it be?**

_____

_____

Why did you choose this word?

_____

_____

What aspects of your personal background or influences on your life have most affected the way you understand the big picture of Revelation?

_____

_____

_____

DISCOVERING THE WAY

During his exile, the apostle John's world was simple. He likely spent his days in prayer and worship, listening to the crashing surf and the birds chirping in the distance as he lived on the tiny island of Patmos, just off of the coast of Asia Minor. Sentenced to a life of exile for preaching the Word of God, John's days were as uneventful and unproductive as the Roman Empire could make them. And for an apostle and witness of Jesus Christ—one sent to preach the gospel—being exiled to a penal colony would have seemed a worse punishment than death.

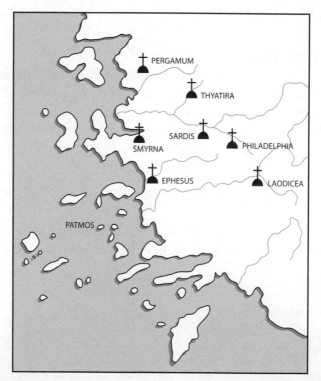

But one day John's uneventful world was interrupted, and he would never be the same. He became known as "John the Seer" because God showed him startling visions that lifted his eyes off of his current circumstances to the person and work of Christ. Through his visions, John became privy to the condition of the churches and the judgments and rewards of the future. On the bleak island of Patmos with no prospects for the future, Christ appeared to John and told him, "Write the things which you have seen, and the things which are, and the things which will take place after these things" (Revelation 1:19).

Can you recall the first time you ever heard somebody teach or preach about biblical prophecy or the book of Revelation? How did you feel? What thoughts came to your mind?

_____

_____

_____

Did this experience make you want to learn more or turn you away from the subject? In what way?

_____

_____

_____

THE THINGS WHICH YOU HAVE SEEN: JESUS CHRIST (REVELATION 1)

After taking in the glorious vision of Christ (Revelation 1:12–16), John was told to write the things he saw (1:19). The very first chapter of Revelation, therefore, records his vision of the Lord Jesus.[1] Throughout the book, and especially in the first chapter, we see that Jesus Christ Himself stands at the center of Revelation. To miss seeing Christ in Revelation is like squinting into the midday sky and missing the sun. His presence radiates everywhere. And you might be surprised to find that Revelation, though it can be a little intimidating at first, will begin to make sense if we keep Christ at the center.

How many times does Revelation 1:1–2 refer to Jesus Christ, either by name or with pronouns like He, Him, or His?

_____

According to these verses, describe the relationship between the revelation John saw and heard and Jesus Christ.

_____

_____

_____

In the following passages, describe how Christ is portrayed.

Revelation 1:5–7

_____

_____

Revelation 1:13–16

_____

_____

Revelation 1:17–18

_____

_____

What is the intended response to John's revelation of Jesus Christ (1:6, 7, 17)?

_____

_____

_____

Though the presence of Christ dominated his past and filled his memories, the apostle John looked forward to seeing Jesus again either at His promised return or upon John's death. Yet in a single moment John's life was interrupted, and his expectations were turned upside down. He found himself first kneeling, then falling down before the Lord Jesus Christ, who then directed John to observe the condition of the seven churches.

THE THINGS WHICH ARE: THE CHURCHES (REVELATION 2–3)

The messages to the seven churches in Revelation 2–3 function almost like job performance reviews—Christ inspected their spiritual condition as they waited for His return. He praised their strengths, pointed out their weaknesses, and warned them to repent or encouraged them to continue in good works. Two of the churches, Sardis and Laodicea, received negative reviews and were called to repent. Two others, Smyrna and Philadelphia, received only glowing praise. The other three—Ephesus, Pergamum, and Thyatira—were each given a mixed report.[2] In general, Christ confronted indifference, the tolerance of gross sin, apathy, and self-sufficiency. His words are hard to hear, but He always offered encouragement and hope.

The first part of Revelation is dedicated to addressing the local churches, showing Christ's obvious concern for the churches' spiritual health during the period between His first and second comings. What does this teach us about our local churches today?

_____

_____

_____

As you evaluate your own involvement with and contribution to your local church, do you think Christ would be mostly pleased or mostly displeased? Why?

_____

_____

_____

The Things Which Will Take Place: The Future (Revelation 4–22)

Having revealed Jesus Christ as the center of the vision (Revelation 1) and the present spiritual condition of the churches during the period of waiting for Christ's return (2–3), Christ then displayed a series of symbolic and prophetic visions of the future (4–22).

When John soared from the mundane island of Patmos through the heavenly doorway (Revelation 4:1), he was thrust into the dazzling, glorious, and majestic presence of God and the never-ending worship that surrounds His throne (4–5). Every part of creation—from the angels nearest the throne to all creatures in heaven and earth—praises the Father, Son, and Holy Spirit.

John's visions reveal the worthy Lamb (Revelation 4–5) and the coming period of Tribulation by which creation is cleansed so that God may draw to Himself as many as will come (6:1–19:5). Through a series of judgments symbolized by seven seals (6; 8:1), seven trumpets (8–9; 11:15–19), and seven bowls (16), we see God moving the world toward the grand climax of Christ's return to destroy evil and usher in righteousness (19:6–20:15). After a thousand years of peace, one final judgment establishes an eternal state, when God redeems humanity and all of creation—a new heaven and new earth (21–22).

Throughout these great movements in the symphony of Revelation, one theme keeps rising to the fore, arranging all the notes into a majestic harmony: Jesus Christ. In the opening vision, He's the Son of Man—the Savior who gave His life for all who believe. In the letters to the churches, He's the head of the church—the One to whom all must reverently submit. In the vision of the throne of God, He's both a lion and a lamb; the only One worthy to reign. In the visions of wrath, He's the righteous Judge who justly punishes sin and rebellion while graciously calling all to repentance and salvation. In the final visions, He's the King of kings and Lord of lords, the One who ultimately eradicates all evil and establishes a kingdom that will endure forever and ever. Without a doubt, the "testimony of Jesus is the spirit of prophecy" (Revelation 19:10).

 Review your one-word answer from "You Are Here" on page 51. What word would you now use to describe the main theme of Revelation?

_____

_____

How does the word you chose earlier relate to this main theme?

_____

_____

_____

CHRIST'S PROMISE TO JOHN ... AND TO US

Although books, movies, and television have portrayed the end times as disturbing events that fit into the horror genre, the book of Revelation actually brings great encouragement to those who know Christ. Why? Because in the end, God wins (Philippians 2:10–11)!

As the spectacular visions of Christ, the churches, future judgments, and the coming kingdom weighed heavily on John's mind, he may have frequently recalled the simple days when he leaned on Jesus's chest at the Last Supper. In the dim light of the Upper Room, mere hours before His suffering and death, Jesus promised His disciples a glorious future.

Read John 14:1–6. What comforting promise did Jesus give to His disciples?

_____

_____

Where was He going (14:2)?

_____

What did He promise to do when He comes again (14:3)?

_____

_____

What must a person do to receive this promise and be comforted by this news (14:1, 6)?

_____

_____

_____

Is your heart troubled today? Why?

_____

How do Jesus's words comfort you? Be specific.

_____

_____

_____

What will happen to believers when Christ returns—when the "dead in Christ" will be raised and the living will be transformed and caught up to God (1 Thessalonians 4:13–18; 1 Corinthians 15:51–53)? According to John 14:2–3, Christ is presently preparing a place for believers in heaven. Therefore, believers will spend some time in heaven before returning to earth to reign. Either way, the point of the passage is clear: we are to be encouraged because Christ is preparing a new, better home for us—and His promise will be fulfilled.

STARTING YOUR JOURNEY

After Christ reminded the disciples of His promised return, He established the service of the Lord's Supper or Communion—a time of recalling our past forgiveness of sins, remembering our present fellowship with Christ and His church, and looking forward to the return of Christ in glory (Matthew 26:26–29). Similarly, the book of Revelation contains these three dimensions: reflection on the past work of Christ, consideration of our current relationship to Christ and the church, and recognition of the coming judgments and rewards. It seems appropriate, then, before we continue on a study of the heart of Revelation, to consider our own past, present, and future in light of the awesome person and work of Jesus Christ.

First, *take this opportunity to look back on the debt Christ paid for your sins.* Every man, woman, and child is in one of two groups in relation to the cross of Christ: those who have personally accepted forgiveness of their sins based on the payment Christ made and those who have not accepted forgiveness and therefore bear their own sin and guilt before God. Where are you?

Have you accepted God's free gift of forgiveness and promise of eternal life? How would you answer God if He were to ask you, "Why should you receive the promises described in Revelation rather than the judgments?"

_____

_____

_____

Read the section, "How to Begin a Relationship with God," located at the back of this book. Does your answer to the previous question differ from the ones presented in that section? If so, how is it different?

_____

_____

_____

Second, *take time to look at your current relationship with Christ and with His church.* A clear relationship exists between our love for Christ and our love for members of the body of Christ, the church. If your relationship to your local church is strained or nonexistent, you may have problems in your personal relationship with Christ.

 Read 1 John 4:7–12, 19–21. According to these verses, how is our relationship with God expressed in our relationships with others?

_____

_____

_____

If we do not have loving fellowship with other believers in the church, what does that say about our relationship with God? Give specific verses from 1 John 4 to support your answer.

_____

_____

_____

Examine your own relationship with others in your local church. Would you consider your relationships to be in harmony, discord, or neutral?

_____

_____

What specific people do you need to reconcile with, or what relationships must you improve, in order to bring about greater fellowship and unity in your church?

_____

_____

_____

Will you commit to do this today? Why, or why not?

_____

_____

_____

Third, *look ahead to Christ's second coming—what does it have in store for you?* If you have already trusted Christ for your salvation and forgiveness of your sins, the wrath of God and judgments of the end times are not for you (1 Thessalonians 1:10; 5:9). However, even believers will face Christ and give account for their conduct while on this earth.

Read 1 Corinthians 3:11–15 and 2 Corinthians 5:9–11. In light of these passages and your answers to the previous questions concerning your relationship to Christ and other believers, are there areas in your life you would be ashamed of before Christ if He were to appear right now?

_____

_____

Write a prayer in your own words asking God to reveal areas of sin in your life that affect your relationship to Christ and the church. Commit to turn away from sin and embrace righteousness by the power of the Holy Spirit.

_____

_____

_____

_____

_____

_____

Are there people in your life who do not yet know Christ personally? If so, list their names here and pray for them throughout this study, asking God to move their hearts so they would respond in faith to the gospel. Commit to praying for them faithfully, knowing that without Christ they will face the judgments described in this book.

_____

_____

_____

_____

_____

⸎

Thank you, Father, for Your work on this earth. Thank You for introducing us to One who has changed the whole course of our lives, given us a new direction, a new purpose, new definition, new reason to go on. Thank You for interrupting our world of sinfulness and selfishness and introducing us to a life of love and joy and forgiveness and peace. I pray today for those who've never met Your Son and ask You to work in their hearts as only You can. . . . Bring them to their knees to faith in Christ alone by Your grace alone.

—Chuck Swindoll

LESSON SIX

RELEASING DEMONS FROM THE ABYSS

Revelation 9:1–12

THE HEART OF THE MATTER

The world-devastating judgments of Revelation appear as three symbols—seals, trumpets, and bowls. In our study of this earthly drama, we have arrived at the fifth of the seven trumpet judgments. At this time, the "abyss" will be unlocked, releasing a host of demons on earth that torment but do not kill humans. The pain will be so severe that people will long to die, but they will not be allowed any form of relief. Even in the midst of this horrific onslaught of demonic forces, we can observe that the spirits of wickedness must submit to the limiting power of the sovereign God.

In preparation for this lesson, read Revelation 9:1–12.

YOU ARE HERE

An invisible war is raging. The warriors strike unsuspecting victims without warning, afflicting them at their weakest moments. Their insidious attacks leave individuals and families reeling in pain and heartache. This war has been rumbling for centuries—even millennia. It's not a war against terrorism, poverty, drugs, or pornography. No, this is spiritual warfare—and every human is in imminent danger of demonic attack.

What do you think of when you hear the term *spiritual warfare*? Be specific. What does this term mean to you? What have you heard or learned about it?

_____

_____

_____

How has Hollywood or other popular media presented demonic forces or Satan? Where do you think they are accurate? Where do you think they are mistaken?

_____

_____

_____

Describe the kind of power that Satan and his demons have in the world today. Is it limited or unlimited? Why?

_____

_____

_____

Can Satan and his demons influence or attack you personally? Is his attack limited or unlimited? Why?

_____

_____

_____

Satan and his demons have been at work tempting and attacking humans since the infamous sneak attack in the Garden of Eden eons ago (Genesis 3). They have never ceased pursuing their ultimate goals of destroying the dignity of humanity and driving a wedge between humans and their Creator. But Revelation 9 shows us that a time will come when the invisible warfare that people experience today will be insignificant compared to the frontal assault of the enemy's army during the Great Tribulation. As we study John's vision and observe the armies of darkness battling in the future, we can better understand how similar spirits of wickedness try to torment us today.

DISCOVERING THE WAY
The dreadful seal judgments unfold in Revelation 6:1–8:6, while the more intense trumpet judgments resound through Revelation 8:7–9:21 and 11:15–19. The bowl judgments—the most severe and cataclysmic of all—appear in Revelation 15:7–16:21. In this lesson, we will consider the effects of the fifth trumpet blast, also called "the first woe" (Revelation 8:13; 9:12). As we examine what prophetic Scripture tells us about the future period of judgment known as the Tribulation, we will witness some of the most sobering scenarios revealed in the Bible.

UNLOCKING THE ABYSS AND RELEASING THE DEMONS (REVELATION 9:1–6)

As soon as the fifth angel sounded his trumpet, John watched a star fall from heaven. The star is often used symbolically in Scripture to refer to a very famous or prominent person (Numbers 24:17), Satan (Isaiah 14:12–17), angelic beings (Job 38:7), human leaders of churches (Revelation 1:20), or even Christ, the "bright morning star" (Revelation 22:16). Some understand the star in this passage to be Satan falling from heaven,[1] though it could simply be a high-ranking demon given authority over the abyss. Either way, the emphasis in this passage is clearly on *what* this star did, not on *who* he is.

GETTING TO THE ROOT
The terms "abyss" and "bottomless" in Revelation 9 come from the same Greek word, *abyssos*. In biblical writings, *abyssos* means "depth" or "underworld,"[2] and can refer to the physical depths of the earth (Genesis 7:11) or to the dwelling place of departed spirits awaiting release or judgment (Romans 10:7; Ephesians 4:8–10; 1 Peter 3:19). Apparently, the abyss is also the place where demons have been kept in prison until judgment (2 Peter 2:4; Luke 8:30–31). Given the context of the end times judgments, it appears that the opening of the abyss in Revelation 9 refers to the short-term release of demons prior to their final judgment.

Read Revelation 9:1–3. According to these verses, what was given to the locusts?

_____

_____

By whom were these things given?

_____

_____

_____

Although we may not like the thought of it, God sometimes uses demons to carry out His purposes—using their evil intentions for God's glory and our good (Romans 8:28). Bible scholar Charles C. Ryrie writes:

> On occasion God may use demons to further His purposes. He sent an evil spirit to stir up the people of Shechem against Abimelech (Jud. 9:23). He used an evil spirit to punish Saul with a mental disturbance that bordered on madness (1 Sam. 16:14). He sent a deceiving spirit to control the prophets and to give Ahab the wrong advice (1 Kings 22:22). He used one to afflict Paul so that he would not become overly proud (2 Cor. 12:7). Because they are creatures, demons are accountable to God and thus can be used by Him as He may desire.[3]

 In Revelation 9:4–5, four limitations are placed on these locust-like creatures. What are they? (Compare your answers to the chart on page 69.)

1. _____

2. _____

3. _____

4. _____

Read Revelation 9:3–6, and note all of the indications that these renegade creatures are still under the sovereign authority of God.

_____

_____

_____

How should this truth encourage us as we encounter spiritual wickedness in the world around us?

_____

_____

_____

DESCRIBING THE LOCUSTS AND THEIR LEADER (REVELATION 9:7–12)

So far we've seen that the power of these creatures is great, but it is utterly limited by God's sovereign hand. He sets the limits, grants permission, and works out His will in spite of the apparent ruthlessness of these fiendish beings. These creatures have been described as "locusts," but the description John provides in verses 7 through 10 reveals that these beings are not members of the animal or insect kingdom—but soldiers in the kingdom of darkness.

DOORWAY TO HISTORY
Locusts and Scorpions

Because of their shocking capacity for devastation, locust swarms were greatly feared by the people of Old Testament times. They inflicted damage on the crops, lands, and basic livelihood of everyone in their path. Entire regions could be stripped by a locust plague: "Areas up to 1000 sq. km. (400 sq. mi.) can be covered by locust swarms, which leave a barren, denuded landscape in their wake. It is easy to see why the locust is identified as one of biblical man's greatest calamities." [4]

Continued on next page

Continued from previous page

Locusts were therefore used as a symbol for horrific judgment, as in the locust-like invading Assyrian army described in the book of Joel. But the locusts that came from the abyss in Revelation 9:3 were far worse than either normal locusts or an invading army. John described these creatures as locusts that were able to sting like scorpions; in fact, they are infamous in the Bible for the excruciating pain inflicted by their stings.[5]

Biblically, locusts and scorpions normally signify severe judgment: "The awesome sight and power of locusts depicted in Revelation 9:3, 7 is beyond anything yet known to man's experience. The author of the book knew well the tradition of locusts as a form of judgment from God."[6]

The demonic locust-scorpion of the end times will not destroy the vegetation of the land like the ancient locust plagues nor kill indiscriminately like an invading army, but they will cause excruciating torment for five months.

Read Revelation 9:7–10. On the left side of the following chart, note the specific words and phrases used to describe these strange creatures. Then, in the right column, record some words that indicate the reactions, emotions, or ideas that each of these symbols bring to mind.

Clearly, the "locusts" are spiritual, demonic creatures—not literal animals or insects. The symbolic representations that John saw were meant to communicate ferociousness, aggression, power, and intelligence. And we can see that this army of wicked spirits is led by a "king." Known as "the angel of the abyss," his name in Hebrew is *Abaddon*, and in the Greek he has the name *Apollyon* (Revelation 9:11). Though some scholars identify this ruler of the abyss as Satan, he is probably a high-ranking lieutenant of Satan who does his dark lord's bidding.[7]

Four Limitations on the Demonic Hoard
1. They cannot hurt the earth's vegetation (9:4).
2. They cannot hurt the 144,000 who have God's seal (9:4).
3. They cannot kill anyone (9:5).
4. They cannot torment longer than five months (9:5).

At the end of this terrible and frightening vision, John gave this ominous warning: "The first woe is past; behold, two woes are still coming after these things" (Revelation 9:12). Though the release of the demons is unspeakably dreadful, the worst is yet to come.

STARTING YOUR JOURNEY

How does the demonic warfare of the future relate to our own spiritual warfare today? Although this section of prophetic Scripture points to events that will take place during a five-month period of the Tribulation, it relates to our lives in four important ways.

First, *we must remember that although they are invisible, demons are real and aggressive.* As long as they have freedom to roam this world, they are in search-and-destroy mode, looking for opportunities to strike both believers and unbelievers.

Second, *we are reminded that although the angels of darkness are innumerable, they are organized and committed to our destruction.* Like a battle-hardened army, Satan's forces know how to wage an efficient war for the hearts and minds of all people. From subtle tricks to a full-blown spiritual *blitzkrieg*, they are ready to use whatever means are necessary to win.

Read 1 Peter 5:8. What does this image suggest about our situation in this world?

_____

_____

_____

What does Jude 8–10 reveal about the power of demons in comparison to our own strength?

_____

_____

_____

Why is it important for us to be aware of demonic forces?

_____

_____

_____

How can ignorance of their activities lead to our harm?

_____

_____

_____

Third, *we should be encouraged that although these demons are powerful and intimidating, they have limitations and can be restrained.* We see that even during the Tribulation, these wicked angels can do only what they are allowed. Today—in the age of the Spirit's restraining power through the church—their power is even more limited (2 Thessalonians 2:6–8).

Fourth, *we must never forget that although these creatures are powerful and insidious, they flee at the sovereign name of the Lord Jesus Christ.* At His matchless name they cower in fear, run for cover, and scramble for survival. With a single syllable of rebuke, Jesus Christ can flatten Satan's entire army. They are no match for Him (Luke 8:26–31).

Read the following passages regarding spiritual warfare. What important truths about spiritual victory do you see in each one?

1 Corinthians 10:13

_____

_____

_____

Ephesians 6:10–17

_____

_____

_____

James 4:6–8

_____

_____

_____

1 Peter 5:6–9

_____

_____

_____

When you're under attack by Satan—through circumstances, temptations, sufferings, or discouragement—how can you be victorious?

_____

_____

_____

_____

Read the unique experience of Paul in 2 Corinthians 12:7–9. What does this tell us about spiritual warfare and the will of God?

_____

_____

_____

_____

In light of this passage, how would you define or describe true, spiritual warfare between believers and Satan? What is our responsibility? What is God's role? Contrast your informed view of spiritual warfare with the various ideas you identified at the very beginning of this lesson in the "You Are Here" section.

_____

_____

_____

_____

_____

_____

_____

_____

Everyone deals with some sort of trial or hardship at any given moment. Some of these are part of the normal hardships of life. Others are brought on by our own sin. Some are temptations of the world. Yet others come from wicked spirits trying to torment or distract us. In every case, the answer is to turn to God—who limits the power of demonic forces and turns their attacks into His victory . . . and ours.

LESSON SEVEN

MORE DEMONS, MORE DEATHS, MORE DEFIANCE

Revelation 9:13–21

THE HEART OF THE MATTER

At the end of Revelation 8 a loud voice announced, "Woe, woe, woe to those who dwell on the earth, because of the remaining blasts of the trumpet of the three angels who are about to sound" (Revelation 8:13). At the blast of the fifth trumpet, we observed the first woe—the release of tormenting demons from the bottomless pit who ravage the hearts and minds of men and women for five months. With the second woe, announced by the sixth trumpet, the intensity of God's judgment increases. Another enormous number of demons is permitted to annihilate one-third of humanity—but those who are left on earth refuse to repent of their wickedness.

In preparation for this lesson, read Revelation 9:13–21.

YOU ARE HERE

When was the last time you worshiped an idol?

Don't think of the shiny, polished gold, silver, or bronze statues made to look like either grotesque demons or beautiful gods. Nor should you consider the paintings or icons used in some corners of Christendom. And few of us would ever bow before relics, bones, graves, or memorials of human beings either living or dead. However, though we may not kiss a cross or exalt an effigy, we are sometimes guilty of idolatry.

Have you observed forms of idolatry in the world around you? What does it look like? Be specific.

_____

_____

_____

What other sins might creep into a person's life after idolatry has taken hold?

_____

_____

_____

What are the effects of idolatry on the Christian life? Provide some personal examples or real-life illustrations.

_____

_____

_____

_____

Carefully consider the following description of idolatry in our culture:

> Idolatry in our society is not so obvious but is just as real as it was in John's day. By definition idolatry is turning an earthly thing into a god and worshiping it rather than the God of creation. Whatever we place ahead of God in our lives is our idol. Therefore, the modern world is replete with idols: money, possessions, power, pleasure, sex, success, fame, drugs. These are all tools of Satan, and there are countless stories in which these very things have tortured and killed those who pursue them. We must warn people of the cosmic powers in control of this secular world and call them to God.[1]

Indeed, the *causes* of idolatry (a rejection of God) and the *effects* of idolatry (a godless lifestyle) ultimately result in the *curse* of idolatry (a rejection *by* God). Most people who become wrapped up in the things of this world—material possessions, people, fame, and fortune—never realize that they are following a path that will result in a hardened heart and a judgment of wrath.

DISCOVERING THE WAY

As we approach the end of the trumpet judgments, we can expect the pitch of wrath to intensify. When the angel sounded the fifth trumpet (Revelation 9:1–12), the locust-like demons were allowed to torment people mercilessly for five months. However, the next judgment brings larger creatures with a deadly attack and catastrophic results. Will the people of the world finally respond to God's resounding call to repentance?

THE FOUR ANGELS ARE PREPARED AND RELEASED (REVELATION 9:13–14)

At the fifth trumpet we witnessed the opening of the abyss and the release of tormenting demons who swarmed the earth like locusts. Upon the blast of the sixth trumpet, we see four angels of death who have been held captive near the Euphrates River (modern-day Iraq). When they are released, all of the forces of hell will break loose across the face of the earth. Step by grueling step, the restraining grace of God is being removed from the world, allowing Satan, his demons, and sinful humans to destroy it . . . and themselves.

According to Revelation 9:13–14, in what part of the world will this particular conflict be centered? Consult a map or other resource to identify the location.

_____

_____

People sometimes read current events into the biblical prophecies regarding this region. Why can this be misleading? What might the effects be when these speculations do not come true? Have you ever been personally affected?

_____

_____

_____

MASSIVE FORCE APPEARS AND KILLS (REVELATION 9:15–19)

The angels of death will unleash absolute carnage throughout the region and the world. Yet even this march of mayhem is under strict limits. God's wrath is under control as He continues to call sinners to repentance.

 Read Revelation 9:15–16 once again. What words or phrases indicate that God is sovereign over the actions of these angels?

_____

_____

_____

In light of the timing of this event, could any part of this prophecy be fulfilled in the present, or must its fulfillment come in the future? Why?

_____

_____

_____

Describe the physical features of this army using the terms found in Revelation 9:17–19.

_____

_____

_____

How many are killed in this judgment?

_____

How are they killed?

_____

_____

_____

Incredibly tragic images fill our minds as we try to imagine the chaos, confusion, grief, and overwhelming shock that will sweep the globe at that time. What humans have experienced in natural disasters, military strikes, and terrorist attacks will be completely forgotten in light of these unparalleled events. Considering that a fourth of mankind was killed during the fourth seal judgment (Revelation 6:7–8) and another third was slain by the massive army in the fifth seal judgment (Revelation 9:13–19), we can estimate that over half of the world's population will be killed by then!

Yet many people will survive this onslaught. What will happen to those who live through it? How will they respond?

THE REST OF HUMANITY SURVIVES WITH AN ATTITUDE OF DEFIANCE (REVELATION 9:20–21)

We would love to imagine that the unbelieving world will see the supernatural events, hear of the cataclysmic disasters, perceive the signs in the heavens, and heed the preaching of the 144,000 missionaries calling for repentance and faith in Christ. We would love to believe that the remaining men and women on the earth will turn from their wicked ways and acknowledge the Father, Son, and Holy Spirit as the one true, triune God, forsaking the idolatrous false religions so rampant throughout the world. Out of love and compassion, we desperately hope that hardship, calamity, and the extreme presence of death will soften the hearts of the lost. But John's vision reveals the opposite to be true. One author evaluates this shocking turn of events:

Those content to give their good days to the devil's service, seldom come to reformation in their evil days. While the pressure of judgment is on them, they may cry, God have mercy!and think to lead a different life; but their vows and prayers vanish with their sorrows, and they are presently where they were before, only the more hardened in their iniquities.[2]

 Read Revelation 9:20–21. From what did the people of earth refuse to repent?

_____

_____

_____

Read Romans 1:18–23. Why is the wrath of God coming upon the world?

_____

_____

What are the root causes of this rampant idolatry?

_____

_____

_____

Read Romans 1:24–32. What were the ultimate results of this idolatrous mentality? How did it affect people's morality and lifestyle? How did it affect their relationships with God?

_____

_____

_____

The great preacher, Donald Barnhouse, puts Revelation 9:13–21 into painful perspective:

> There is no evidence in the Bible; there is no evidence in history; and now there is no evidence in prophecy which would indicate that men have ever been brought to God in great numbers through tribulation. One-third of the race may die, but the other two-thirds do not for that reason move toward God. Reluctantly we are forced to accept the verdict, "There is none that understandeth, there is none that seeketh after God" (Rom. 3:11).[3]

DOORWAY TO HISTORY
Idolatry in the Ancient World

Idolatry characterized nearly every other non-Christian and non-Jewish religion in the ancient world. In fact, if your god could not be seen, it was not regarded as a god at all. Pagan idolaters actually regarded Jews and Christians as "atheists" because they did not believe in a god they could see. One Bible encyclopedia summarizes the situation of idolatry in the New Testament world: "Idols were venerated in temples dedicated to the traditional gentile gods, in popular magic and superstition, as well as in the mystery religions and in emperor worship."[4]

Many of the immoral practices condemned in Revelation 9:20–21 were often associated with idolatry and idolatrous religions. In the New Testament, where the emphasis was on an internal conversion rather than external actions, idolatry could be viewed as an attitude rather than merely an action. So the practice of idolatry condemned in the Old Testament "is widened to include anything that leads to the dethronement of God from the heart."[5]

STARTING YOUR JOURNEY

When we stand beside the apostle John and through his vision witness the devastating impact of the future judgments, we may glean lessons that affect us in the present. Two specific truths arise from the vision of the sixth trumpet.

First, *no matter how impressive human strength may be, the presence of supernatural activity is overpowering*. Without temporal protection, we're helpless. We focused on the matter of demonic activity more fully in the previous lesson and learned that only when we turn to God for protection from demonic attacks can we hope to stand victorious in the battle that is raging around us.

Second, *no matter how extensive human suffering may be, the curse of spiritual depravity is overwhelming*. Eugene Peterson's translation of Revelation 9:20–21 helps describe this point in modern terms:

> The remaining men and women who weren't killed . . . went on their merry way—didn't change their way of life, didn't quit worshiping demons, didn't quit centering their lives around lumps of gold and silver and brass, hunks of stone and wood that couldn't see or hear or move. There wasn't a sign of a change of heart. They plunged right on in their murderous, occult, promiscuous, and thieving ways. (Revelation 9:20–21 MSG)

Idolatry of various forms stands at the heart of their rebellion against God, leading to greater sin and defiance even in the midst of His obvious judgment and His merciful calls to repentance and salvation. Idolatry blinds humanity to the Word of God. However, we must keep in mind that modern forms of idolatry can negatively affect our own personal relationships with God, causing us to be distracted from Him and hardening our hearts to the Holy Spirit.

 Read Ephesians 5:5–6 and Colossians 3:5–6. What types of behavior are associated with idolatry? What are the ultimate effects of idolatry?

_____

_____

_____

The short book of 1 John ends with the final exhortation, "Little children, guard yourselves from idols" (1 John 5:21). Until that point in the letter, the word *idol* was never mentioned. Read 1 John 5:19–20. Given this context, what do you think John meant when he offered this instruction? Which "idols" was he referring to?

_____

_____

_____

Recall your answer to the very first question in this lesson—noting the forms that idolatry takes today. Identify three areas of your life in which you may have a tendency to put other things or people above God. Consider your addictions, priorities, and pursuits—even if they may appear to be neutral or even healthy choices.

_____

_____

_____

In light of this lesson, what could happen to your relationship with God if you do not turn from these areas of idolatry? Be specific.

_____

_____

_____

Write a prayer of repentance, asking God to forgive you and deliver you from these idols that are hijacking your attention from the one true God. What will you do to loosen the potential stranglehold that they have on your life?

_____

_____

_____

_____

_____

_____

_____

❦

In this lesson we observed that the sin of idolatry—worshiping things other than the one true God—caused such a hardening of people's hearts against God that even His most extreme judgments were unable to capture the world's attention and incite repentance. But idolatry is not just a sin that enslaves the unsaved during the Tribulation. It is also a strong temptation for believers today. Are material things, people, or pursuits slowly hardening your heart to the spiritual things of God? If so, consider the warning of Revelation and repent.

LESSON EIGHT

A STRONG ANGEL, A STRANGE ASSIGNMENT

Revelation 10:1–11

THE HEART OF THE MATTER

The intensifying message of judgment rising from every page of the book of Revelation can be overwhelming. However, God provides a few interludes along the way. Each intermission allows the reader to pause, take stock of what has happened, and prepare for what is to come. The first interlude between the sixth and seventh seals revealed the existence and experiences of two groups of redeemed believers during the Tribulation (Revelation 7). Beginning in Revelation 10, the second interlude interrupts the sequence between the sixth and seventh trumpets. This intermission functions as a reminder that God's judgment has both positive and negative aspects.

In preparation for this lesson, read Revelation 10:1–11.

YOU ARE HERE

Epic stories affect us at an emotional level, where the impact and meaning goes beyond what mere words can describe. They draw us in to a running narrative, where we may become a part of the action, a victim of the conflict, or a victor with the conqueror. Some of the greatest novels and movies of our day—though fictional—reveal powerful truths about humanity, redemption, grace, and justice. They illustrate heroism, illuminate defeat, and resonate with real emotions. And therein lies the real power behind myths, legends, and other epic stories both ancient and modern.

Christian author John Eldredge notes three truths that surface in every good story, including God's true story of creation and redemption: first, "things are not what they seem;" second, "this is a world at war;" and third, "we have a crucial role to play." [1]

The book of Revelation tells a story. Though it utilizes symbols and paints word pictures, the story it tells is true. It reveals real events that will happen in the future (Revelation 1:1). However, its spiritual truth transcends time and applies to us even today.

 Reflecting on your study so far, describe how the book of Revelation teaches that "things are not what they seem."

_____

_____

_____

Even though the fulfillment of John's visions will take place in the future, how does Revelation communicate that we live in a "world at war"?

_____

_____

_____

What do you think Revelation suggests is our "crucial role to play" in its story? Why does God want us to know and understand both these truths and the role we play related to them?

_____

_____

_____

DISCOVERING THE WAY

As the story of the book of Revelation unfolds like a great drama spanning heaven and earth, we may recognize each of the three truths of a great story within it. First, "things are not as they seem"—although we dwell in a physical reality, an unseen realm also exists that will become even more apparent in the future. Second, "this is a world at war"—the classic conflict between good and evil has been raging since the fall of Satan. And right in the midst of it all, "we have a crucial role to play." This is no place for spectators. Like it or not, our very presence on this earth dictates our involvement.

ANOTHER NECESSARY INTERLUDE

In every play or concert, listeners and performers alike need an intermission. On long journeys travelers require a rest stop for refreshment. Even the biblical psalms of praise contain a periodic *Selah* to mark a time for transition and reflection. Thankfully, the book of Revelation has occasional interludes designed to help us pause and catch our breath in the midst of disturbing and even frightening scenes of judgment.

When did the first interlude in Revelation take place?

_____

What events took place during that first interlude? What truth did it reveal about the end times?

_____

_____

_____

In the interlude between the sixth and seventh trumpets (Revelation 10:1–11:14), we experience a change in emphasis from the outpouring of judgment and wrath on unbelievers to the consolation and encouragement of believers. At the same time, the apostle John is recommissioned in his prophetic role.

THE ANGEL ON EARTH AND THE VOICE IN HEAVEN
(REVELATION 10:1–4)

As the blast from the sixth trumpet and the thunderous hoofbeats of a massive, demonic army faded into the distance, John found his attention turned upward as a magnificent angel descended from heaven bearing further revelations from God.

How is the angel described in Revelation 10:1–3?

_____

_____

_____

What is John instructed to do after he hears the seven peals of thunder?

_____

_____

_____

According to Genesis 9:13–16, what might the rainbow in Revelation 10:1 symbolize?

_____

_____

If this is indeed the intended significance of the rainbow, what might it suggest about the meaning of Revelation 10 as a whole?

_____

_____

_____

Read Daniel 8:26 and 12:4, 9. What does it mean to "seal up" a vision or prophecy? How does this action limit our ability to have a complete understanding of the end times?

_____

_____

_____

_____

What does this truth reveal regarding teachers who might claim to know the exact timing of the end times or specific identifications of places, people, and events?

_____

_____

_____

_____

THE ANGEL'S ANNOUNCEMENT (REVELATION 10:5–7)

With this announcement, God reminded John that the coming judgments are part of His perfect plan. He predicted them long ago, and they function as an intentional step toward a greater good.

 In your own words, describe the content of the strong angel's proclamation (Revelation 10:5–7).

_____

_____

_____

Read Amos 3:6–8 and Romans 1:18. According to these verses, to what might the "mystery of God . . . as He preached to His servants the prophets" refer?

_____

_____

_____

Is this mystery good news or bad news? Explain your answer.

_____

_____

_____

John Walvoord explained the "mystery" of Revelation 10:7 this way:

> This mystery had been previously announced to God's prophets. The reference, therefore, is not to hidden truth but to the fulfillment of many Old Testament passages which refer to the glorious return of the Son of God and the establishment of His kingdom of righteousness and peace on the earth. While God's purposes are not necessarily revealed in current events where Satan is allowed power and manifestation, the time will come when Satan no longer will be in power and the predictions of the Old Testament prophets will be fulfilled.[2]

Recall Revelation 6:10, when the Tribulation martyrs called out, "How long, O Lord, holy and true, will You refrain from judging and avenging our blood on those who dwell on the earth?" The mighty angel of Revelation 10 announces that God's response to those prayers will soon be coming to an end. The final number of the redeemed will be fulfilled, and the judgment of the wicked will be complete.

The second part of this interlude moves to focus on John's role in this heavenly drama. God has given him a vital part in the proceedings.

John's Strange Assignment (Revelation 10:8–11)

As the great angel fell silent, the booming voice from heaven gave John a strange—but very significant—assignment: Eat the little book (Revelation 10:8–9)! Though the angel warned John that the book would taste sweet in his mouth and make his stomach sour, by this time in his life John had learned to instantly obey the command of the Lord. So John did exactly as he was told (10:10). His consumption of the little book symbolizes the complete appropriation of the prophetic message.

Read Ezekiel 2:8–3:4. To whom was Ezekiel's message of judgment directed?

_____

_____

On the other hand, to whom is John's message of judgment sent (Revelation 10:11)?

_____

_____

Who would be likely to receive this message as good news? And who would consider this message to be bad news? Why?

_____

_____

_____

DIGGING DEEPER
Should Christians Take Pleasure in God's Wrath?

Many Christians struggle to relate to the martyrs' calls for vengeance against their persecutors in Revelation 6:10 or even to the pleas for judgment by David in several Old Testament psalms (for example, Psalm 3, 7, 12, and others). Indeed, believers who are called to follow Christ and embrace the spirit of the Sermon on the Mount (Matthew 5) may have a hard time reconciling pleasure in God's wrath and delight in His mercy. However, as illustrated by John's experience with the little book, the truths we believe and the gospel message we preach have sweet *and* sour elements.

One evangelical commentator summarizes this well:

> John and other Christian prophets actually take pleasure in God's pronouncement of judgment (1) because God's word expresses his holy will, which will ultimately make even events of woe redound to his glory (11:17–18; 14:7; 15:3–4; 19:1–2); (2) because God's righteousness, justice, and holiness are demonstrated when he punishes sin; (3) because punishment of the church's persecutors vindicates Christians and reveals that they have been in the right all along, contrary to the world's verdict (cf. 6:9–11; 18:4–7). Saints are even depicted in 19:1–4 as shouting "hallelujah" when God executes his judgment. Finally, (4) the expansion of 10:8–11 in 11:1–13 shows that part of the message about judgment is an encouragement to the faithful to endure in loyalty to God's word, which is a message of sweetness to John. Nevertheless, Christians, like God, do not take sardonic pleasure in the pain of punishment as an end in itself apart from the broader framework of justice.[3]

Understanding this background, why do you think the message of the little book was both sweet and sour to John?

_____

_____

_____

What does this tell us about our own attitudes toward judgment?

_____

_____

_____

STARTING YOUR JOURNEY

The interlude in Revelation 10 reinforces the fact that things in this world are not what they seem. Believers know there's a war going on and that at any moment the sporadic attacks and brief skirmishes in the battle between good and evil will erupt into the worst spiritual and physical conflict in history. Yet God emphasizes another truth in Revelation 10. The apostle John had a crucial role to play — proclaiming the mystery of God to "many peoples and nations and tongues and kings" (Revelation 10:11).

Just like John, we also have roles to play in God's ultimate plan. Though we can't call ourselves "apostles" and though we don't receive visions and revelations from God or swallow prophetic books to utter inspired words, each of us has been given a crucial mission to share the gospel with the world (Matthew 28:19–20). But first we must internalize the message — allowing it to become a part of our hearts and minds.

This goal leads to three important truths that apply to us today. First, *much of God's truth tastes sweet and is pleasant to hear.* However, whether or not it tastes sweet depends solely on our response to God. Those who know Him and have trusted Him for salvation should have no fear of coming judgments. Be encouraged by the reality of God's promises and hopeful for the future.

Read the following passages regarding our security and protection in Christ, and then select at least one to memorize.

John 3:16–18

John 10:28–30

Romans 8:1–2

Romans 8:35–39

1 Thessalonians 5:9–11

Revelation 3:10–12

Second, *some of God's plans are hard to accept.* His judgments, trials, and afflictions are bitter for those who have no hope in God. Many cannot see or understand God's greater good as it will be ultimately accomplished through these events. They live in a world filled with fear and hopelessness.

 In the following passages, describe how Christ's message can have either a positive or negative effect on those who hear it.

John 9:39

_____

_____

2 Corinthians 2:15–16

_____

_____

1 Peter 2:6–10

_____

_____

Have you witnessed both of these responses to the gospel? Give a few specific examples.

_____

_____

_____

Finally, *all of God's ways are right and reliable, and we can trust Him.* Because God is sovereign, nothing is ever out of His control. And because He is good, we can be confident that He will use all things—even the deeds of evil men—to accomplish His ultimate purpose. Job's words resound with this truth: "Shall we indeed accept good from God and not accept adversity?" (2:10).

The gospel of Jesus Christ involves both bad news and good news. Although the gift of God's salvation by grace through faith is good news to those who trust Christ, it is bad news for those who refuse a personal relationship with Him. Therefore, we must not only understand and accept the gospel ourselves, but also be able to explain the message to others.

In your own words, explain the bad news and the good news of the message of Jesus Christ. If you need help, read "How to Begin a Relationship with God" at the end of this book.

_____

_____

_____

_____

_____

_____

What is your particular role in sharing Jesus Christ with the world? How has God uniquely gifted you to contribute to this mission of the church? Have you responded to His call and command?

_____

_____

_____

_____

_____

What will you do this week to engage in the crucial role God has given you?

_____

_____

_____

_____

❦

In this lesson we observed that God's unfolding story of judgment and redemption reveals an unseen spiritual realm—things are not as they seem. A war is raging for the souls of all people. Each one of us has been given a crucial role in communicating God's messages of judgment and grace. Have you accepted God's commission on your life? Or, like John, are you ready for a recommission from God? Will you respond to Him today?

LESSON NINE

TWO FEARLESS, FUTURE WITNESSES

Revelation 11:1–14

THE HEART OF THE MATTER

The second interlude in the Revelation drama continues. After assimilating the prophetic scroll of judgment (Revelation 10:9–10), John continued to record the amazing things he saw and heard, and he was also given the unusual job of measuring the temple and those who worship in it. Then, in Revelation 11, we are introduced to two extremely powerful and courageous witnesses who take center stage and prophesy during part of the Tribulation. Because of God's protection, the two witnesses are impervious to harm and preserved from death as they announce further judgment. Following their time of ministry, the protective shield about them is lifted, and they are killed—but what occurs after their death is nothing short of miraculous. It truly demonstrates God's ability to turn tragedy into triumph.

In preparation for this lesson, read Revelation 11:1–14.

YOU ARE HERE

Classic stories often portray average individuals who overcome overwhelming adversity to accomplish unimaginable goals. Such tales inspire and motivate us to transcend our own weaknesses and accomplish great things. Enemies attack; obstacles are thrown into their paths; tragedies strike—but the heroes of great stories find a secret source of strength from beyond themselves that enables them to vanquish the most potent adversaries.

What are some cinematic or literary examples of people who overcome unbelievable challenges before emerging victoriously?

_____

_____

_____

Why do you think people are moved or inspired by such stories?

_____

_____

_____

Describe a real-life example of this kind of story.

_____

_____

_____

What is it about this particular true story that attracts you?

_____

_____

_____

 DISCOVERING THE WAY

The interlude begun in Revelation 10 continues into Revelation 11, where John zooms in for a close-up at the epicenter of end-times activity: Jerusalem. We see the rebuilt temple rising from its ancient ruins. We watch the ministry of two men who—by God's special empowerment—defy all the powers of the world to preach a message of judgment. And we observe the ominous rumblings of greater judgment still to come. Step by agonizing step, the promises of God to His people begin to unfold before our very eyes as we catch a sneak peek of God's final drama.

MEASURING THE TEMPLE IN JERUSALEM (REVELATION 11:1–2)

Gripping action scenes in movies often begin with an initial, context-establishing shot—a distant image of a building, a city, or even a planet—intended to help the audience understand the setting and context within which the events of the scene are about to take place. Revelation 11:1–2 is one such context-establishing shot—it helps us to understand the events that follow.

Read the following passages regarding the temple and the Tribulation. Write out each of these passages in your own words. What will happen to the temple during the Tribulation?

Daniel 9:26–27; 12:11

_____

_____

_____

Matthew 24:15–16

_____

_____

_____

2 Thessalonians 2:3–4

_____

_____

_____

Bible scholar Charles Ryrie suggests that the temple mentioned in Revelation 11:1–2 is "the temple that will be built during the Tribulation, in which Jewish worship will be carried on during the first part of that seven-year period and in which, at the midpoint, the man of sin will exalt himself to be worshiped."[1] The temple will be rebuilt during a time of unparalleled tension, and this period will end in outright warfare (Revelation 11:2). By the way, it is likely that the forty-two-month time period looks forward to the second half of the seven-year Tribulation—the reign of the Beast—which will be discussed more fully in Revelation 13.

GOD'S TWO WITNESSES (REVELATION 11:3–12)

 Read Revelation 11:3. How does the context-establishing shot in Revelation 11:1–2 help us understand the context in which the two witnesses will be prophesying? Describe some of the challenges they may face.

_____

_____

_____

 According to Revelation 11:5–6, what special powers will God grant to the two witnesses? How long will they have these powers?

_____

_____

_____

What will happen after the witnesses finish prophesying (11:7–8)?

_____

_____

_____

Describe the response of the people of the world (11:9–10).

_____

_____

_____

Like the Lord Jesus Christ centuries before them, these two witnesses will be rejected and killed. Then they will be resurrected and taken up into heaven. This parallels Jesus's resurrection and ascension. However, though the witnesses' experiences are somewhat similar to Jesus's life, the book of Revelation records some significant differences. For example, after His resurrection, Jesus Christ appeared in bodily form to a little more than five hundred hand-picked witnesses (1 Corinthians 15:1–8), resulting in the eventual conversion of millions of people worldwide. In contrast, the resurrection of the two witnesses will be seen by *all* people remaining on the earth, resulting in the salvation of very few (Revelation 11:11–12).

 DIGGING DEEPER
The Two Witnesses
"May I see some identification?"

This question may be the first one readers ask when they encounter individuals in the book of Revelation. The two witnesses in Revelation 11:3–12 are no exception, and they have been identified in a variety of ways. Some have identified the witnesses as Moses and Elijah coming back from the dead. Others identified them as Enoch and Elijah. Those who believe that this particular part of Revelation refers to events that occurred in the first century have identified the two witnesses as Peter and Paul, James and John, or even two high priests that were killed by the Romans in AD 68.[2]

We have very few specifics about these two individuals. We know they are given authority to prophesy for three and a half years, during which time they are protected from harm and given special power to call down plagues and judgments (Revelation 11:3–6).[3] Because the symbols of the two olive trees and two lampstands in Revelation 11:4 correspond directly to the symbols representing Zerubbabel and Joshua in Zechariah 4:3–14, it may be that their testimony will somehow relate to the rebuilding of the temple in Jerusalem as mentioned in Revelation 11:1–2. Most importantly, the miraculous authority given to the two witnesses by God is similar to that of Moses, Elijah, and other Old Testament prophets, demonstrating the critical nature of their ministry during the future Tribulation.

In the end, we must exercise prudence and say that we simply do not know the exact identity of these two witnesses. To try to name them would be to go beyond what is actually written in the Scriptures into rampant speculation. Biblical scholar Grant Osborne is probably correct when he says, "These are the two major eschatological [end times] figures expected in the last days, and that is sufficient for this context."[4]

The authority given to the two witnesses resembles that which was given to Old Testament prophets as they called the nation of Israel back to God. Look back at Revelation 11:5–6, and then read the following passages. Note which powers of the two witnesses are shared by these prophets.

Exodus 7:17

_____

1 Kings 17:1

_____

_____

2 Kings 1:10–12

_____

_____

Jeremiah 5:14–15

_____

_____

What might these parallels tell us about the nature of the two witnesses' ministry and message? Why do you think their message will be so poorly received?

_____

_____

_____

The two end-times witnesses provide God's final announcement of the coming kingdom. Like John the Baptist and Jesus in the first century, these two witnesses will announce, "Repent, for the kingdom of heaven is at hand" (Matthew 3:2; 4:17).

At the completion of the two witnesses' ministry, the fate of those who remain will be sealed as the final trumpet sounds and the final judgments commence. Revelation 11:7–14 details the various responses to the ministry, death, and resurrection of the two martyrs:

- In utter rage, the Beast will attack and kill them. (11:7)

- The people of the world will rejoice over their deaths. (11:9–10)

- Blinding fear will overcome those enemies who witness their resurrection. (11:11–12)

- Those who are left on the earth will fear and give glory to God. (11:13–14)

The ministry of these two witnesses will certainly leave a profound mark on the lives of those who witness their exploits. Every friend and enemy of God will respond in some way to their testimony. Yet as we examine their lives, we see that they have no basis for personal boasting. Their preservation, their miraculous powers, their message — everything that sets them apart comes from the sovereign hand of God. When their mission is over, their power will come to an end. However, God does not abandon His vessels. Instead, He turns tragedy into triumph, ushering the witnesses into His heavenly presence.

MORE DEATHS . . . MORE TO COME (REVELATION 11:13–14)

At the conclusion of their ministry, while the world still gawks at the shocking events of the resurrection and ascension of the two witnesses, the city of Jerusalem rumbles violently with an earthquake, causing a tenth of the city to fall and seven thousand people to die (Revelation 11:13).

In verse 13, who does "the rest" refer to? Does this verse necessarily mean that all the rest repented and were saved? Why, or why not?

_____

_____

_____

Is it possible for unbelievers to give glory to God and yet refuse to repent and turn to Him? Can you think of other examples of this response, either in the Bible or in your own experience?

_____

_____

_____

Revelation 11:14 tells us that the second woe announced back in 8:13 has come to pass. The great earthquake following the death and resurrection of the two witnesses marks the end of an era. The window of repentance is closing quickly, and the time for the final judgments is swiftly advancing.

In the first interlude we saw that God would seal and mobilize 144,000 Hebrew believers to evangelize the world and eventually compose the remnant of Israelites who survive the Tribulation and populate the future kingdom (Revelation 7:1–8). In this second interlude we watched God work through another "remnant"—two witnesses who carry out an overwhelming task in spite of unbelievable adversity.

God often works through a remnant, and He always equips them with the power and fortitude they need to accomplish His will.

He will do the same for us.

 STARTING YOUR JOURNEY
God's unchanging plan remains in motion and on target. When His hand empowers a person's life and ministry, that ministry will continue on until He brings it to completion. Even death cannot stop the legacy of a faithful minister of God. While it may be possible to silence the voice of one who bears witness to the truth, the truth that has been proclaimed is indestructible.

One major truth for today emerges from the account of the two witnesses: *God transforms tragic situations into triumphant events*. Underdogs become overcomers. Weakness is changed into strength. Overwhelming obstacles are magnificent opportunities for God to display His presence and power.

Today positive thinkers and motivational speakers try to inspire us to accomplish great things, embrace our potential, and achieve our goals . . . in our own strength. Many Christian leaders advocate a life of personal success, health, wealth, and happiness. Yet when we contrast this "me-centered" philosophy with the heroes of the Bible and the saints of history who accomplished great things *for God in His power*, both the motivation and the outcome are completely different. The glory is God's—not ours.

Consider the worldly motivations and philosophies that have crept into Christian thinking. What are they? How are they different from the successful ministry of the two witnesses in Revelation 11?

_____

_____

_____

What worldly attitudes and actions have affected your own view about personal success and accomplishments? Be specific.

_____

_____

_____

The Bible is filled with examples where God uses outcasts and underdogs to accomplish His will. He seems to delight in turning the tables on the world's mindset of "bigger is better" and "only the strong survive."

Read the following passages, and note what they teach about God's ability to overcome our weaknesses and to accomplish great things through apparently limited means.

Isaiah 52:13–53:12

_____

_____

_____

1 Corinthians 1:25–31

_____

_____

_____

2 Corinthians 12:7–10

_____

_____

_____

Hebrews 11:32–40

_____

_____

_____

Study one or two of these great stories as part of your Bible study over the next week, focusing on the weakness or tragedy of the person's life, how God used or overcame this handicap, and what great things He accomplished through this person. Keep a journal of your observations.

Moses (Exodus 1:1–12:41)

Gideon (Judges 6–8)

Samson (Judges 13–16)

Ruth (Ruth 1–4)

David (1 Samuel 16–31)

Esther (Esther 1–10)

Daniel (Daniel 1–6)

Looking back over your life, what have been your greatest obstacles, tragedies, or disappointments? How have you responded to them?

_____

_____

_____

_____

_____

    Of the principles you discovered in this lesson, which ones relate most to your current weaknesses and challenges? How will you respond to future challenges or obstacles?

_____

_____

_____

_____

_____

⚜

In a world that sets worldly success and accomplishments as the ultimate standard for determining a person's worth, it's easy to forget that God often chooses the small over the large and the small-in-number over the masses. Scripture is replete with examples: David and Goliath . . . Elijah and the prophets of Baal . . . Gideon's three hundred and thousands of Midianites . . . Esther and Haman. God is in the business of transforming otherwise tragic situations into triumph. Are you ready for God to turn your obstacles into opportunities?

LESSON TEN

THE SOUNDING OF THE SEVENTH TRUMPET

Revelation 11:15–19

THE HEART OF THE MATTER
The series of seven seals, trumpets, and bowls in the book of Revelation precedes the enthronement of Christ as King of kings and Lord of lords over His future earthly kingdom. It represents God's promise to complete His work of reclaiming creation from the wicked adversary and usurper, Satan. And it also reminds us that while we eagerly await the coming of the King, we should be about the work of His faithful servants.

In preparation for this lesson, read Revelation 11:15–19.

YOU ARE HERE
Every single day, Christians throughout the world recite one of the most familiar prayers from Scripture in hundreds of languages. The prayer begins with two familiar words: *Vater unser . . . Pater noster . . . Notre père . . . Pater hēmōn . . . Padre nostro . . . Our Father*. Many churches have incorporated the Lord's Prayer of Matthew 6:9–13 into their worship services. This tradition goes all the way back to the first century when Christians would recite the Lord's Prayer three times every day.[1] In fact, by the time John wrote the book of Revelation, reciting the Lord's Prayer as a regular part of worship was likely a widespread practice. Interestingly, though the faithful have offered that prayer to God daily since the founding of the church, most of that ancient prayer has not yet been answered.

Read Matthew 6:9–13. What did Christ tell us to pray for in verse 10?

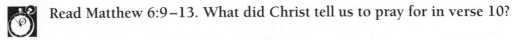

_____

_____

_____

What would the world look like if this part of the Lord's Prayer was already answered? Literally? Spiritually?

_____

_____

_____

Though believers are engaged in advancing the spiritual kingdom of God through preaching the gospel (Acts 28:31; Colossians 1:13), the day is coming when all aspects of the Lord's Prayer will be fulfilled quite literally (Revelation 11:15–19). Christ will reign over all the earth, the world will be transformed, sin and death will be eradicated, and finally, God's purposes will be accomplished on earth and in heaven.

DISCOVERING THE WAY

A trumpet blast, booming voices, and a celestial chorus resound before a heavenly temple. Flashes of lightning, claps of thunder, shuddering earthquakes, and damaging hail cover the earth. After a short interlude, Revelation 11:15–19 returns to the drama of the final judgments. With the sound of the seventh trumpet, God prepared John for the seven dreadful bowls of wrath, painting a brief, panoramic scene of events, focusing not on His judgment and wrath but on His glory and sovereignty.

THE LOUD ANNOUNCEMENT FROM HEAVEN (REVELATION 11:15)

The loud voices of praise from heaven refer to future events in the past tense because the future reign of Christ over the earth is absolutely certain. The events described in Revelation 11:15–19 await fulfillment at God's final judgment and second coming of Christ.

Read Revelation 11:15. How is the Lord's Prayer literally fulfilled in this passage?

_____

_____

_____

Chronologically, the seventh trumpet both introduces and includes the final period of God's wrath, the seven bowls. Commentator John Walvoord writes, "The fact that this will be fulfilled at the Second Coming makes it clear that the period of the seventh trumpet chronologically reaches to Christ's return. Therefore the seventh trumpet introduces and includes the seven bowl judgments of the wrath of God revealed in chapter 16."[2] In Revelation 12–16, we will observe more details of the final three-and-a-half years of the Tribulation as the effects of the seventh trumpet are played out on the earthly stage.

The mention of the kingdom of God and of Christ in Revelation 11:15 refers back to prophecies of the messianic reign found throughout Scripture. Read the following passages, and note what each one says about the Messiah's coming reign.

Genesis 49:10	
1 Chronicles 17:11–14	
Isaiah 9:6–7	
Daniel 2:44	
Daniel 7:13–14	
Luke 1:30–33	

DIGGING DEEPER
The Last Trumpet and the Seventh Trumpet

Some scholars equate the "last trumpet" announcing the rapture of the church in 1 Corinthians 15:52 with the seventh trumpet of Revelation 11:15. However, a close examination reveals that these two trumpets refer to separate events.

The seventh trumpet of Revelation 11:15 announces the final phase of the wrath of God, the beginning of Christ's reign, and the praises of the heavenly chorus in response to this exchange of power. In contrast, Paul's trumpet of 1 Corinthians 15:52 refers to the bodily resurrection and the "catching up" of believing saints.

We must also remember that Paul wrote 1 Corinthians around AD 55, and therefore he would not have known about the seven trumpets of John described in Revelation, because it was written around AD 90. And if John's seventh trumpet was meant to refer us back to Paul's last trumpet, John probably would have used the term *last trumpet* to make this connection. And he would likely have mentioned the resurrection or rapture.

It is best to regard these two trumpets as distinct symbols used to refer to separate events in God's future plan.

Using the following chart, list the events that take place in relation to the trumpets in each of these three passages.

1 Corinthians 15:51–52	1 Thessalonians 4:14–17	Revelation 11:15–19

What similarities do you see between 1 Thessalonians 4:14–17 and
1 Corinthians 15:51–52?

_____

_____

_____

Based on these similarities, how confident are you that Paul was referring to
the same future event in these two passages? Circle your choice.

Very confident   Somewhat confident   Not very confident   Not at all confident

Besides the mention of a trumpet, what similarities do you see between the
events described in Paul's passages and the events of Revelation 11:15–19?

_____

_____

_____

Based on the similarities or differences, how confident are you that
Revelation 11:15–19 is referring to the same future event as the other two
passages? Circle your choice.

Very confident   Somewhat confident   Not very confident   Not at all confident

What difference would your answers to these questions make in regard to
your understanding of the timing of the rapture of the church? What practical
difference should this make in your life?

_____

_____

_____

WORSHIPFUL RESPONSE AMONG THOSE IN HEAVEN (REVELATION 11:16–18)

When the seventh angel sounded his trumpet, the voices of heaven broke forth in praise. The age-old prayer of the church, "Your kingdom come," will now be fulfilled: "The kingdom of the world has become the kingdom of our Lord and of His Christ; and He will reign forever and ever" (Revelation 11:15). Finally, the kingdom prophecies that span both the Old and New Testaments will be realized.

In John's vision, these events are viewed as already accomplished, but we should not let this fact confuse us. From our perspective, all of the events described in this passage are yet future. However, because the purposes of God cannot change and the prophesied events are certain, we can join in the heavenly throng and praise God for what He *will* do.

 GETTING TO THE ROOT
"So I'm driving along, and I see this sofa in the middle of the road. . . ."

When we tell stories that happened to us in the past, we often switch to the present tense because it makes the story more vivid. The Bible also uses different tenses for dramatic effect. In prophecies, authors sometimes refer to future events with past tenses. Isaiah 53, which refers to the coming of Christ, is a good example of this practice. Though the prophecy was written around 700 BC, it referred to the events of Christ's life in the past tense. From our vantage point, the songs of praise in Revelation 11:15–18 could be viewed in "prophetic past tense"—the fulfillment of Christ's reign is so certain, it can be expressed as if it has already been accomplished. One Hebrew scholar notes: "[The] abrupt appearance [of this tense] in this capacity imparts to descriptions of the future a forcible and expressive touch of reality, and reproduces vividly the certainty with which the occurrence of a yet future event is contemplated by the speaker." [3]

Based on Revelation 11:16–18, list each of the distinct events referred to by the voices of praise.

_____

_____

_____

How do those in heaven respond to these events?

_____

_____

_____

How should we respond to the certainty of the reign of Christ and the judgment of the earth? Be specific.

_____

_____

_____

The seventh trumpet guarantees a victory in which the kingdom of this world will become the kingdom of God and Jesus Christ. Nations will be enraged and rebel, but they will ultimately be defeated as Christ and His saints take their seats to reign (Revelation 20:4–6). No matter what the world looks like today; no matter how out of control things appear; in the end, God wins! Never forget that essential truth.

SIGNIFICANT MESSAGES COMING OUT OF HEAVEN (REVELATION 11:19)

In the beginning of this chapter, John was told to measure the temple of God on earth (Revelation 11:1). At the end, John returns to a temple, but this time it's the temple of God in heaven (Revelation 11:19). The temple in heaven indicates unbroken fellowship with God—it is open to all. Within this temple John saw the ark of the covenant. This symbol of God's holiness and justice is also the basis for His wrath. God keeps the covenant and never forgets its provisions. Because of His mercy and grace, God grants complete access to His throne to those who believe. Yet on the basis of His unalterable standards of law and justice, He exercises wrath and judgment on unbelievers.

Christ told His disciples to pray, "Your kingdom come. Your will be done, on earth as it is in heaven" (Matthew 6:10). When we look heavenward, we see the model of how things should be on earth. One day this ideal will be real; faith will become sight; the hidden will be revealed. In the meantime, we can live our lives with confidence in the sovereign goodness of God.

STARTING YOUR JOURNEY

As we reflect on the panoramic foretaste of future events announced by the seventh trumpet, two relevant truths come to the surface.

First, *we have unlimited access to God by His grace.* The image of the open temple in heaven (Revelation 11:19) communicates to us that believers stand in an open relationship with God because of His grace and mercy. Based on the forgiveness bought for us by the blood of Jesus Christ, we can have confidence as we approach Him. And as His beloved children, we are free from His coming wrath (1 Thessalonians 1:9–10; Revelation 3:10). Christians will never experience the seventh trumpet judgment—nor any of the trumpets in Revelation. Instead, they will have already been transformed and taken to heaven at Paul's "last trumpet" (1 Thessalonians 4:16); preparing to return with Christ and reign with Him (Revelation 17:14; 19:14).

Have you personally accepted God's free gift of eternal life? Do you know for sure that you will have access to God and be free from the coming wrath? If you're unsure, read the "How to Begin a Relationship with God" section at the end of this book.

In your own words, explain what you must do to be saved.

_____

_____

_____

_____

_____

Read Hebrews 4:16. What is your greatest need today? Have you boldly approached God's throne, or are you cowering from Him in fear? Compose a prayer, communicating your need and asking for God's intervention in your life.

_____

_____

_____

The second relevant truth that can be drawn from this lesson is that *our sovereign King will reign and reward us*. John considers this truth to be so clear and so certain that he uses the past tense to declare it. Our response should be one of trust and confidence in this hope, as well as taking part in diligent service until He returns.

Based on the following passages, how does Christ's *current* position of authority affect our actions today? In other words, what are we supposed to be doing in light of His exalted position?

Matthew 28:18–20

_____

_____

_____

Acts 1:6–8

_____

_____

_____

Romans 14:10–13

_____

_____

_____

Hebrews 3:12–14

_____

_____

_____

In what ways are you personally working at these tasks? Be specific.

_____

_____

_____

Read Romans 14:6–9, 1 Corinthians 3:10–15, and 2 Corinthians 5:9–10. How are these passages meant to motivate us to greater service?

_____

_____

_____

❧

In this lesson we heard the seventh trumpet announce the coming reign of Christ, the judgment of the world, and the reward of believers. John's vision in Revelation 11:15–19 should call every person to a decision. Unbelievers are called to respond in faith and submission to the coming King . . . or face judgment. Believers are called to preach the gospel of Jesus Christ until He comes and to prepare themselves to reign with Him in the kingdom. Though believers will not suffer the judgment and wrath foreshadowed by the seventh trumpet, they will be held accountable for their service of the King. How will you respond to God's final trumpet blast?

EXPOSING THE ULTIMATE EVIL EMPIRE

Revelation 12

THE HEART OF THE MATTER

As the curtain opens on Revelation 12, the archenemy of God's people takes center stage. The spiritual battle that had been happening behind the scenes is now on display, exposing the strategy of Satan's evil empire. But we need to be careful, thoughtful, and discerning in our study. Because so much of the truth revealed in this chapter is set forth in colorful, vivid symbols, we don't want to misinterpret what they represent or miss the big picture of what they portray.

In preparation for this lesson, read Revelation 12:1–17.

YOU ARE HERE

We only have to remember movies like *Oh, God!* or *Bruce Almighty* to conclude that popular culture holds an often twisted view of God. Whether He's portrayed as a wisecracking old man or a wise old custodian—certainly Hollywood gets it wrong more often than they get it right.

God is not the only victim of popular caricatures. Satan, too, is often portrayed in ways that twist the truth, creating fear when there should be confidence or false confidence when there should be fear.

 How has Satan been portrayed in movies or popular culture? Give some specific examples.

_____

_____

_____

How do these examples portray Satan's powers? His limitations?

_____

_____

_____

How do these examples suggest Satan can be defeated?

_____

_____

_____

In what ways do you think the world is right in its interpretation? Where has the world distorted the true picture?

_____

_____

_____

 DISCOVERING THE WAY

Satan hates you. He would want nothing more than to sabotage your love for God and love for others, to tempt you into a moral catastrophe, or to see you choose sin rather than righteousness. And when you falter, he stands ready to accuse you before God.

Most often his methods are indirect—establishing and fortifying moral pitfalls and traps in the world to lure, snare, and destroy unsuspecting victims. Sometimes his methods are more direct—bringing made-to-order temptations into our lives to ensnare us. And if God were to allow it, Satan would unleash his entire arsenal against humanity, marching both spiritual and physical armies across the face of the earth to destroy all men and women.

Satan's ultimate evil empire has been spreading its influence for millennia. Masquerading as an attractive angel of light (2 Corinthians 11:14), Satan rarely exposes his demonic empire to the light of truth. However, a day is coming when God will remove His restraining power from the earth, and Satan will be allowed to run amok for a brief time. Deception, destruction, and despair will ravage the planet. But even then Satan's acts will be those of a desperate villain, for he knows his time is short.

TWO COMMON ERRORS CONCERNING SATANIC ATTACKS

Down through the ages people have played into the hands of the Adversary by falling into two errors in their thinking about him. The first error is to believe that a literal Satan and literal demons do not exist. The second error is to believe that Satan stands behind every temptation, sin, or evil event. Satan relishes these two errors: believing he is everywhere and refusing to see him at all.

C. S. Lewis, in his classic work, *The Screwtape Letters*, mentions both extremes:

> There are two equal and opposite errors into which our race can fall
> about the devils. One is to disbelieve in their existence. The other is to
> believe, and to feel an excessive and unhealthy interest in them. They
> themselves are equally pleased by both errors, and hail a materialist or
> a magician with the same delight.[1]

 What dangers are involved in seeing Satan everywhere and believing that he is working behind every negative person or event?

_____

_____

_____

What dangers are involved in refusing to believe that Satan exists or that he is merely a symbol for personal or societal evil?

_____

_____

_____

Do you tend toward one of these extremes? If so, which one? Why?

_____

_____

_____

Understanding that Satan is neither all-powerful nor completely powerless will help us understand the real challenges we face as we do battle against the evil empire. Yet it is also important to understand that his ability to unleash his full fury and hatred on God's people is limited in the present age. But one day Satan's empire will be allowed to strike the world in full force before God's coming kingdom causes it to crumble.

THREE MAJOR CHARACTERS (REVELATION 12:1–6)

Before the seventh trumpet initiated the final series of bowl judgments on the earth, John saw a remarkable panorama of events spanning thousands of years. In Revelation 11 we saw a slideshow of events from the future Tribulation, culminating in the praises of heaven at the prospect of Christ's reign. In Revelation 12, John recorded his vision of the behind-the-scenes conflict that will rage between the kingdom of God and Satan's evil empire.

However, much of Revelation 12 is written in signs and symbols that need to be interpreted before we can understand the future events they portray. Especially important are the three main characters: the Woman, the Dragon, and the Male Child.

> **DIGGING DEEPER**
> *The Cast of Characters in Revelation 12–13*
> The vision described in Revelation 12–13 involves a cast of seven characters that play out a panoramic drama which spans at least two thousand years of past and future events. An understanding of the symbolic characters will help us to understand the significance of this sweeping drama in God's plan of redemption.

Symbolic Character	Literal Identification	Explanation and Interpretation	Other Symbols with Similar Meaning in Revelation
Woman	The remnant of Israel	The key identification is found in Genesis 37:9–10, where the same symbols are used to represent the twelve tribes of Israel. However, it's best to see the Woman as representing the remnant (elect) described by Paul in Romans 9:1–8 rather than all of ethnic Israel.	144,000 elect (Revelation 7:1–8; 14:1–5)
Dragon	Satan	The symbol of the seven heads and ten horns corresponds with the same number of heads and horns in Daniel's beast-like representations of the nations that opposed Israel in the Old Testament — Babylon, Medo-Persia, Greece, and Rome (Daniel 7). Satan has always used ungodly nations in his attempts to destroy God's people.	Devil (Revelation 12:9)
Male Child	Christ	The Male Child is identified as the One who will "rule all nations with a rod of iron" (Revelation 12:5). This is a messianic reference similar to Psalm 2:9 and Revelation 19:15. Though Satan sought to destroy Him, Christ ultimately triumphed.	The Lamb that was slain (Revelation 5:6), the Lion of Judah (5:5), King of kings and Lord of lords (19:16)
Offspring	Tribulation saints	While the Woman (the remnant of Israel) will be protected, the "rest of her offspring," all believers in Christ during the Tribulation, will suffer persecution and death.	The martyrs (Revelation 6:9–11) and the "great multitude" (Revelation 7:9–17)
Michael and his angels	Archangel Michael and the elect angels	Michael is described as "one of the chief princes" who stands guard over Israel and battles demonic forces for God's people. He squared off with Satan over Moses's body (Daniel 10:13, 21; 12:1; Jude 9).	None
First Beast	Antichrist	This end-times dictator and persecutor of Israel is described in both the Old Testament (Daniel 7:8, 11, 23–26; 9:26–27; 11:36–12:3) and the New Testament (2 Thessalonians 2:3–12). He will be the individual leader of a massive empire, empowered by Satan, and committed to destroying all of God's people.	None
Second Beast	False Prophet	The Antichrist's religious and spiritual guru or chief lieutenant, the false prophet helps bolster the Antichrist's authority by coercing and forcing the world to worship the Beast and the Dragon in a worldwide system of false religion (2 Thessalonians 2:9–12).	None

Read Revelation 12:1–6. Based on this passage, who do you think are represented by the Woman, the Dragon, and the Male Child?

_____

_____

_____

Historically, did Satan try to destroy Christ before His resurrection? In what ways?

_____

_____

_____

Read Psalm 2, Revelation 12:5, and Revelation 19:11–16. Who will fulfill the promise of ruling with a rod of iron?

_____

According to Revelation 2:26–27, who else will share in this rule?

_____

Are you among the group described in Revelation 2:26–27? If not, or if you are unsure, read the "How To Begin a Relationship with God" section at the end of this book.

_____

Two Great Conflicts (Revelation 12:7–17)

Revelation 12 predicts two great conflicts—one in heaven and the other on earth. In the first conflict, we observe a clash between Satan and the archangel Michael (Revelation 12:7–8). Michael, who has been defending God's people for millennia

(Daniel 10:13, 21), defeats the armies of Satan in heaven and casts them down to the earth. This future event will probably occur at the beginning of the seven-year Tribulation, at the same time as the rapture.

Although popular ideas of Satan imagine him as the king of hell ruling over demonic servants and damned sinners, this is not true according to the Bible. Walvoord notes: "While the concept of Satan in heaven is difficult to comprehend, it is clear that he is now the accuser of saints (cf. Job 1:6; Rev. 12:10). Though Satan was defeated at the first coming of Christ (John 16:11), his execution was delayed and is in stages."[2] Satan currently has limited access to both heaven and earth, but his banishment to the abyss and ultimate consignment to the lake of fire will occur at the end of the Tribulation (Revelation 20:1–10).

 Read the words of the loud voice in heaven in Revelation 12:10–12. Why are those who dwell in heaven called to rejoice?

_____

_____

_____

Why does the voice pronounce "woe" on those who dwell on the earth?

_____

_____

_____

How is Revelation 12:10–12 an appropriate exclamation if this event occurs immediately after the rapture of the church as described in 1 Thessalonians 4:16–17? Who would be dwelling in the heavens? Who would be dwelling on the earth?

_____

_____

_____

When Satan and his demons are cast out of heaven, several key changes will result. First, he will no longer be able to accuse God's people. Second, Satan will no longer have access to the presence of God to gain permission to test and tempt. Third, the horrors of earthly evil will increase. Even as cries of victory resound from heaven, earthly woes ring out as Satan desperately tries to inflict as much damage as possible during his final countdown to ultimate defeat.

Immediately after Satan is thrown down, he will attempt to erase Israel from the face of the earth (Revelation 12:13). It should be no surprise that the Jews and the people of the nation of Israel have been the object of his attacks even until our own day. Many rulers and nations want nothing else than to destroy Israel and all Jews permanently.

However, in the end times, God will continue to preserve the nation from harm. In Revelation 7:1–8 God sealed 144,000 Jews for physical and spiritual protection during the Tribulation. They are represented by the symbol of the Woman in Revelation 12. She is given supernatural protection from Satan's military attack, which is signified by a flood from the Dragon's mouth (Revelation 12:14–16).

These events will take place during the first three and a half years of the seven-year Tribulation. At the end of this period, Satan changes his plan of attack: "So the dragon was enraged with the Woman [the remnant of Israel], and went off to make war with the rest of her children [the tribulation saints and martyrs], who keep the commandments of God and hold to the testimony of Jesus" (Revelation 12:17).

What new madness will Satan use to make war with the saints? We will examine his tactics in the next lesson, when we will study Revelation 13.

STARTING YOUR JOURNEY

Through the vivid descriptions of Revelation 12, we witness an incredible series of dramatic events that pan heaven and earth, spanning thousands of years. Yet the great epic begun in chapter 12 and concluded in chapter 13 introduces a few practical points that will help us in our everyday lives.

First, Revelation 12 teaches us that *Israel may be blind and disobedient as a nation, but God has never forgotten them*. He never will. His reputation as a promise-keeper is at stake. God will remember His people and preserve them. He will protect them as persecution arises, and ultimately His promises will be fulfilled.

Recall both positive and negative examples of current international attitudes toward Jews in general and the nation of Israel in particular.

_____

_____

_____

Although most ethnic Israelis have not accepted Jesus as their Messiah, God has still preserved them as a distinct people over the last two thousand years. What does this fact tell us about His faithfulness to Christians who may not live up to their Christian testimony?

_____

_____

_____

Second, Revelation 12 teaches us that *although Satan is a powerful and aggressive foe, he will not triumph.* Satan accuses us before God every day and night (Revelation 12:10), while at the same time Jesus Christ, who is our advocate, intercedes for us. One day God will resurrect the saints and transform the living, giving them new, immortal bodies. On that day Satan's mouth will be shut, for he will no longer have any basis to accuse us. When that happens, he will be cast out of heaven, and the countdown to his execution will begin.

As you examine your own life, what sins could Satan accuse you of today?

_____

_____

_____

Read Romans 8:1–3; Romans 8:33–37; and 1 John 2:1. Why aren't believers condemned for their sins?

_____

_____

_____

In the list of sins you identified on the previous page, mark through each one and write above it: "Paid in full." Then pray to God, thanking Him that Satan cannot bring these charges against you because all your sins—past, present, and future—have been paid for by the sacrifice of Jesus Christ.

Third, Revelation 12 shows us that *we may be open and assaulted targets today, but we need not fear*. The events of Revelation 12 have not yet come to pass, so Satan is still under the restraint of God's hand. However, even during the Tribulation, Satan's time will be short, and he will do only what God allows. We need not fear!

Read the following passages that encourage us to stand firmly and fearlessly in the face of spiritual attacks. Select one or more of the following passages to memorize.

Luke 22:31–32

Ephesians 6:12–13

2 Timothy 1:7

1 Peter 5:8–10

James 4:7–8

1 John 4:4

Although Satan roams heaven and earth today making accusations against God's people and throwing traps and snares in their paths, he is a creature standing under condemnation and awaiting final destruction. We must remember that even his most diabolical schemes must be submitted to the sovereignty of God. In light of this truth, believers can feel confident in God, who promises to be faithful to preserve His people against Satan's inevitable attacks both now and in the future. Satan's earthly triumph will be short-lived, but our own triumph through Christ is eternal.

LESSON TWELVE

ANTICHRIST: THE BEAST OUT OF THE SEA

Revelation 13:1–10

THE HEART OF THE MATTER
Since the birth of Christianity, faithful believers have expected a coming evil dictator who would have an enormous evil influence over the entire world, deriving his power from none other than Satan himself. Revealed in Scripture under various titles, the Antichrist's clearest and most definitive description is found in the first ten verses of Revelation 13. This powerful man will emerge on the world stage like a "beast coming up out of the sea" (Revelation 13:1). He will be the most persuasive and dynamic political and military leader history has ever seen. Though believers today need not fear this embodiment of evil, Scripture warns us that the "spirit of antichrist" has long been at work in the world.

In preparation for this lesson, read Revelation 13:1–10.

YOU ARE HERE
The most significant ingredient in any political movement is leadership. Success is completely dependent upon the choice of a leader. Good leaders understand and embody the beliefs and goals of the movement. They can correctly identify problems, provide solid solutions, and carry out the right course of action to produce desired results.

 Give an example from history or experience in which a great leader achieved objectives that benefited people for generations.

_____

_____

_____

What were some character traits or skills that helped him or her achieve these objectives?

_____

_____

_____

How did people—including critics—respond to this person?

_____

_____

_____

Now consider a negative leader—such as a dictator or tyrant—who sought to achieve evil goals. How did he or she gain power?

_____

_____

_____

Why did people follow him or her?

_____

_____

_____

What was the result of his or her rule for the people who followed? For the rest of the world?

_____

_____

_____

Wicked people in powerful positions can harness and ignite the fallen state of humanity in shocking ways. Without a dictator named Hitler, there would have been no Holocaust; without Idi Amin, no Ugandan genocide; without Pol Pot, no killing fields; without Osama bin Laden, no September 11.

In order for Satan to carry out his insidious regime of world domination, he will use a powerful and popular dictator. Though this magnanimous maleficent was mentioned briefly in Revelation 11:7 as the murderer of the two witnesses, we meet him in person for the first time in Revelation 13:1–10.

 DISCOVERING THE WAY
Anybody who has had even limited exposure to the topic of the end times will be familiar with the Antichrist. Hollywood has painted strange pictures of this diabolical figure. Bible scholars from the earliest decades of the church have tried to describe what his reign would be like. And down through the ages religious and political leaders have been labeled "Antichrist" in the heat of debate.

 What do you think the Antichrist will be like? In the following space, write a character profile or job description for the future Antichrist.

_____

_____

_____

Besides the Bible, where have your ideas about the Antichrist come from?

_____

_____

_____

Though we see the first symbolic vision of the Antichrist in Revelation 13, this apocalyptic figure is no stranger to Scripture. The apostles John and Paul both referred to this man in conjunction with the end times.

Read 1 John 2:18–22; 4:2–3; and 2 John 1:7. How did John describe the Antichrist in these passages?

_____

_____

_____

Read 2 Thessalonians 2:3–12. How did Paul describe the "man of lawlessness" in this passage?

_____

_____

_____

Do these passages refer to the Antichrist as a person in the past, present, or future? Explain your answer.

_____

_____

_____

The Old Testament also describes the Antichrist in Daniel 7:24–26 and 9:26–27. In light of these passages from Daniel and the previous passages from Paul and John, how would you change the character profile you wrote earlier?

_____

_____

_____

Although the rise of the Antichrist, as described in Revelation 13:1–10, will take place at a literal, future date during the Tribulation, the New Testament tells us that the "spirit of antichrist" or the "spirit of lawlessness" is already at work in the world through the activities of Satan. Though believers need not fear the dictator of the end times, we can learn to recognize the present manifestations of the "spirit of antichrist" by looking carefully at the future Antichrist—the literal embodiment of the ultimate Enemy of God's people.

THE ANTICHRIST'S POWER AND AUTHORITY
(REVELATION 13:1–2)

The previous lesson ended with a dramatic cliff-hanger. The Dragon (Satan) was in desperate pursuit of the Woman (Israel) but had experienced repeated frustration as he attempted to destroy her. Revelation 12:17 chronicles Satan's change of focus from the supernaturally protected people of Israel to the "rest of her children, who keep the commandments of God and hold to the testimony of Jesus." Now, in Revelation 13, we see the means by which Satan will attempt to annihilate those who believe in Christ during the Great Tribulation—the Antichrist.

 Read Revelation 13:1–2. Note all of the descriptive elements that make up this symbolic Beast.

_____

_____

_____

From where does the Antichrist receive his power and authority?

_____

The exotic—even bizarre—symbols used to describe the Beast are not just frightening features conjured up to illustrate the monstrous character of the Antichrist. The vision of the Beast is drawn from specific images in the book of Daniel in order to communicate the reality of this end-times dictator.

In Daniel 7, Daniel had a vision of a series of four beasts rising from the sea—the first like a lion, the second like a bear, the third like a four-headed leopard, and the fourth "dreadful and terrifying and extremely strong" with ten horns (Daniel 7:3–8). J. Dwight Pentecost rightly interprets these four beasts of Daniel for us as the successive ancient empires who opposed Israel: Babylon, Medo-Persia, Greece, and Rome.[1] If we add up the number of heads and horns on the four beasts in Daniel 7, they equal the seven heads and ten horns of the Beast in Revelation 13.

John Walvoord explains the symbolism of the Beast: "In Revelation 13:2 the beast was seen to gather in the symbolism of the three preceding empires— Greece (a leopard, cf. Dan. 7:6), Medo-Persia (a bear, cf. Dan. 7:5), and Babylon (a lion, cf. Dan. 7:4)."[2] This symbolism suggests that the Antichrist of the future Tribulation will embody the sum total of all the world empires that oppose God and His people. He will be directly empowered by Satan himself, acting as the ultimate dictator and leading the ultimate evil empire.

THE ANTICHRIST'S UNIVERSAL APPEAL (REVELATION 13:3–4)

The meaning of Revelation 13:3 has been greatly debated for centuries.[3] Some have said the "fatal wound" refers metaphorically to the kingdom of the Beast—that he suffers a deadly political blow and survives. However, the Greek phrase translated "as if it had been slain" is the same phrase that is used to describe the Lamb of God—Jesus—whose death was clearly real and resulted in a literal, bodily resurrection (Revelation 5:6). Therefore, because we have identified the Beast as the Antichrist of the end times who is described in terms of his world empire, we should conclude that Revelation 13:3 points to his physical death and "miraculous" resuscitation.

According to Revelation 13:4–5, how will the world respond to the healing of the Antichrist's fatal wound?

_____

_____

_____

In today's world of advanced medicine and technology, what kind of astounding event do you think would need to occur to elicit such a widespread response?

_____

_____

_____

THE ANTICHRIST'S EVIL ACTIVITIES (REVELATION 13:5–8)

Once the Antichrist has captured the attention of the whole world through the deceptive miracles of Satan and has gained complete authority above all earthly rulers, his totalitarian regime could accurately be described as "hell on earth." And, if even the believer's tongue can be metaphorically "set on fire by hell" (James 3:6), we can only imagine the hellish words that will spew from the mouth of Satan's personal pawn. His motives, methods, and manner of deception will be fueled by the unrestrained power of Satan. The Antichrist will truly be the personification of evil.

 After reading the description of the nature of the Antichrist's words and deeds in Revelation 13:5–8, list several modern-day examples of this same "spirit of antichrist" at work in our world.

_____

_____

_____

The Antichrist will glory in a fanatical following of wild-eyed zealots from every tribe, language, people, and nation. Only believers—those who have had their names written in the Lamb's book of life—will resist his mesmerizing deception. Everybody else will worship him like a god and give him their unquestioned loyalty!

THE ANTICHRIST'S PERSECUTION OF BELIEVERS (REVELATION 13:9–10)

Those who refuse to worship the Beast will suffer severely. Revelation 13:9–10 admonishes the reader to snap to attention and heed a solemn warning: "If anyone has an ear, let him hear. If anyone is destined for captivity, to captivity he goes; if anyone kills with the sword, with the sword he must be killed. Here is the perseverance and the faith of the saints."

For a moment, try to imagine yourself as one of those faithful saints during those terrible days. They will sometimes huddle together for mutual defense, and sometimes they will stand alone before their persecutors. How might they feel during their time of trial? How will they endure? Revelation 13:10 tells us that they may be taken captive or killed. Revelation 6:11 acknowledges that a set number of believers will be killed as martyrs during this period of time. Clearly, this persecution will require great perseverance and faith among the saints.

 STARTING YOUR JOURNEY
Although the monstrous reign of the Beast will take place during the future Tribulation, a study of this end-times dictator should remind us of some helpful realities about the "spirit of antichrist" that is already at work in the world.

First, *satanic wonders are often impressive, but they are always deceptive*. People and events are not always what they seem. Be alert and discerning!

Have you ever been the victim of spiritual deception? How did it happen? What might you have done to prevent it? What actions can you take to prevent yourself from falling for this type of deception in the future?

_____

_____

_____

Does Satan attempt to deceive through false miracles today? In what ways? Explain your answer.

_____

_____

_____

Second, *wherever anything or anyone other than God is worshiped, Satan is pleased.* He doesn't care if you worship your possessions, your money, your job, your family, or yourself. Remember, Satan's goal is to keep people from worshiping God.

Take a moment to examine your life. What have you placed before God? Return to your answers in the "Starting Your Journey" section of Lesson 7. Have you made progress in removing the bondage of idolatry from your life? How? What steps might still be necessary?

_____

_____

_____

Third, *when Satan's power is at its worst, God's power is at its best.* When a messenger of Satan came to torment Paul with a "thorn in the flesh" (2 Corinthians 12:7), he called out to God and asked Him to remove this physical ailment. Yet God responded, "My grace is sufficient for you, for power is perfected in weakness" (2 Corinthians 12:9). God allowed the thorn to remain—as a reminder of His power and for the purpose of His glory.

What would you say is the most painful or difficult attack by the "spirit of antichrist" you have experienced? Briefly describe the situation here.

_____

_____

_____

How has this experience frustrated or hindered you?

_____

_____

_____

Read 2 Corinthians 12:7–10. Have you asked the Lord to remove this hindrance? Why, or why not?

_____

If God chooses not to remove this difficulty from you, how should you respond? In prayer, ask God to help you respond this way by His grace.

_____

_____

_____

_____

⌘

In this lesson we observed the many signs of the spirit of antichrist that are present in the world today, including false signs and wonders, blasphemies, misdirected worship, and persecution of believers. Most of us have been touched in one way or another by the torments of these precursors. Because the spirit of antichrist is empowered by Satan, we don't stand a chance against its deception and destruction without depending entirely on the power of God to rescue and preserve us. You can trust God to protect you from the spirit of antichrist in the world. He is our ultimate protector.

LESSON THIRTEEN

ANTICHRIST'S LIEUTENANT:
THE BEAST OUT OF THE EARTH

Revelation 13:11–18

THE HEART OF THE MATTER

The pages of Scripture are bursting with warnings about false prophets and teachers. Revelation 13 describes two end-times deceivers: one is a future political leader, the Antichrist (Revelation 13:1–10); the other is his chief lieutenant—the most powerful false prophet of all time—who will force the world to worship the Antichrist. Even today, Satan uses various people—especially religious leaders—to spread his lies under a brilliant cloak of trickery. To counter his deceptive ways, we must wield God's weapons of wisdom, knowledge, and discernment.

In preparation for this lesson, read Revelation 13:11–18.

YOU ARE HERE

Over the course of our lives, we have probably been victimized by a con artist or bamboozled by a charlatan at one time or another. However, of all the cons we might fall prey to, the most destructive deception comes from a religious fake who deals in counterfeit truth.

Recall a time when you were deceived by someone with malicious intent, especially in the religious arena. Describe the circumstances in detail.

_____

_____

_____

When you discovered the truth, how did you feel about the person who deceived you?

_____

_____

How did you feel about yourself?

_____

_____

What might have prevented this deception?

_____

_____

_____

 DISCOVERING THE WAY
Revelation 12 ended with Satan frantically seeking to destroy God's people, having been frustrated in his vicious attempts to wipe Israel off the map. Then, in Revelation 13:1–10, we witnessed the rise of a political and military dictator, the Antichrist. However, Satan's most sinister and destructive weapon against mankind is about to appear on the earthly stage: the Antichrist's lieutenant—a master of *religious deception*.

SATAN'S CONSUMING PLAN AND OBJECTIVE

Few things delight the devil more than religious deception. Of his entire arsenal of attack, he relishes lies and deceit above all else. In his consuming plan of spiritual seduction, he uses a number of means—people, philosophies, religions—whatever it takes to confuse and distract people from their devotion to Christ.

Read 2 Corinthians 11:2–4. What intimate relationship does this passage use to describe the believer's devotion to Christ?

_____

_____

_____

Read Revelation 13:13–15. How does Satan seek to distract and deceive us? What ploys does he commonly use?

_____

_____

_____

Read the following warning passages, and note the details concerning the character and methods of false prophets and teachers. Then, in the summary box below your observations, write a general definition of false prophets and teachers, incorporating your observations from these passages.

Passage	Character and Methods
Jeremiah 14:14	
Matthew 7:15–20	
Mark 13:22	
2 Corinthians 11:13–15	
Galatians 1:6–9	
2 Peter 2:1–3	
1 John 4:1–3	
	Summary

Though satanic deception is real and present today, the full force of Satan's power will be revealed in the coming Tribulation. Revelation 13:11–18 opens the curtain to unveil the personification of religious deception—the Beast from the earth or "false prophet" (Revelation 16:13; 19:20).

THE FALSE PROPHET'S IDENTITY AND AUTHORITY (REVELATION 13:11–13)

 Read Revelation 13:11–13. Note at least seven characteristics or actions of the second Beast that you observe in these verses.

_____

_____

_____

What is significant about the fact that the False Prophet resembles a lamb but speaks like a dragon?

_____

_____

_____

How do the signs described in verse 13 resemble the signs of God's true prophets in 1 Kings 18:37–39 and Revelation 11:5–6?

_____

_____

_____

How does this description of the False Prophet compare with the ways in which Satan tries to deceive people today?

_____

_____

_____

THE FALSE PROPHET'S STRATEGY (REVELATION 13:14–15)

In the midst of the worldwide chaos caused by natural disasters, political upheavals, and widespread death, the False Prophet will present a deceptive, fake religion to a world starving for hope.

 Read Revelation 13:14–15. How will people all over the world respond to the False Prophet?

What will the False Prophet do to accomplish his goal?

_____

_____

_____

The Greek verb translated as "deceives" in Revelation 13:14 comes from *planaō*, which means "cause to wander" or "lead astray."[2] Our English word *planet* comes from the same root—the ancient world looked into the night sky and saw a few wandering stars among a consistent field of sparkling constellations. One might wish that Satan's deceptions would affect only a small handful among millions, but the reality should boggle the mind: the False Prophet of the end times will deceive the majority of the world through his hellish antics.

The world will fall prey to the second Beast's deceptive message and methods. One commentator notes:

> His arguments will be subtle, convincing, and appealing. His oratory
> will be hypnotic, for he will be able to move the masses to tears or
> whip them into a frenzy. He will control the communication media of
> the world and will skillfully organize mass publicity to promote his
> ends. He will be the master of every promotional device and public
> relations gimmick. He will manage the truth with guile beyond words,
> bending it, twisting it, and distorting it. Public opinion will be his to
> command. He will mold world thought and shape human opinion
> like so much potter's clay. His deadly appeal will lie in the fact that
> what he says will sound so right, so sensible, so exactly what unregen-
> erate men have always wanted to hear.[3]

 As you read the preceding description of the False Prophet's deception, what modern-day examples of similar deceptive methods came to mind?

_____

_____

_____

_____

Although from our vantage point we have no way of knowing *exactly* what the "image of the beast" mentioned in Revelation 13:15 will be like, we can clearly discern what its effects on the world will be at that time. Everything—from miracles to massacres, from words to wars—will focus the people of the world toward worship of the Antichrist.

THE FALSE PROPHET'S ECONOMY (REVELATION 13:16–18)

During this period of time, people will still need to buy and sell, to earn a living, and to provide for their families. The Antichrist and False Prophet will strike their most severe and horrific blow at the level of basic necessities.

 Read Revelation 13:16–17. Disregarding the actual nature of the mark, what do you observe regarding the purpose and function of this mark in the Antichrist's world order? What does it signify? What are the ramifications for refusing it?

_____

_____

_____

How have books, movies, and other media presented this mark? Are these speculative or reasonable? Why?

_____

_____

_____

How do these presentations compare with what we can glean directly from Scripture? Are they similar? Or different?

_____

_____

_____

DOORWAY TO HISTORY
Will the Real Antichrist Please Stand Up?

Throughout history people have tried to identify the man behind the mark: tagging an individual as the Beast or False Prophet of Revelation 13. One commentator aptly notes, "The number of the beast down through the centuries has been linked with literally hundreds of different possibilities."[4] In Latin, Greek, and Hebrew, letters stand for numbers, so anyone with a calculator and some creativity can paste the "666" label on a number of prominent personalities. The following men have been seriously proposed as being the villain of the end times:

- Titus Flavius Vespasian
- Nero Caesar
- Mohammed
- Constantine
- The popes
- Martin Luther
- Napoleon Bonaparte
- Abraham Lincoln
- Adolf Hitler
- Benito Mussolini
- John F. Kennedy
- Ronald Reagan
- Mikhail Gorbachev
- Saddam Hussein
- Osama bin Laden

As it turns out, none of these men completely fulfilled the job description of Revelation 13. The truth is, we cannot know who the Antichrist will be until he is already in—and out of—control (2 Thessalonians 2:6–8).

Clearly, the commerce of the future will revolve around this identifying mark, whatever it may be. Possessing the mark will prove one's allegiance to the Antichrist; refusing the mark will demonstrate faith in Jesus Christ. Perhaps no other time in history will delineate the identity of Christians so clearly. And in that day, the questions and riddles revolving around the identity of the Beast, the nature of the mark, and the calculation of the number 666 will be answered for those who possess divine wisdom and discernment (Revelation 13:18).

STARTING YOUR JOURNEY
With the introduction of the False Prophet in Revelation 13:11–18,
religious deception in the flesh will strut across the stage of worldwide
history. What appears to be true will be false. What seems valid will be
invalid. His lamb-like gentleness will lead to public persecution and brutality. The
amazing signs and wonders will end in a supernatural lure that draws in all but those
who place their trust in Jesus Christ.

Though Satan is unable to unleash the full force of his deception in the present
age, the same types of deceit he uses are currently present among us. Just as one
person will ultimately become the False Prophet in the end times, there have been
and will continue to be precursors to the False Prophet in the world and in the
church today.

We desperately need discernment in order to stand firm in the midst of spiritual
deception. Merriam-Webster's defines *discernment* as "the quality of being able to
grasp and comprehend what is obscure." [5] Like a hound discovering hidden contra-
band, discernment sniffs out deception. But in the face of powerful satanic deceit, the
level of discernment required of us can only come from the overwhelming power and
wisdom of God.

**Read 2 Peter 2:1–3, and list at least ten observations regarding the characteris-
tics or actions of false teachers.**

_____

_____

_____

Which of these do you feel may be most alluring to you personally? Why?

_____

_____

_____

According to Philippians 1:9–11 and Hebrews 5:13–14, why is discernment a vital tool for believers to develop? How does it help us to avoid spiritual deception?

_____

_____

_____

    In Revelation 13:18, John called for wisdom above all else to keep believers from becoming victims of satanic deception. Do you consider yourself to be a wise person? Why, or why not?

_____

_____

_____

What does each one of the following passages teach about the wisdom and knowledge believers have in Christ?

    1 Corinthians 2:10–16

_____

_____

    Ephesians 1:8–9, 17

_____

_____

    James 1:5; 3:17

_____

_____

1 John 2:20, 27

_____

_____

   What must you do to develop knowledge, wisdom, and discernment in your own life? List several specific steps you intend to take right away.

_____

_____

_____

_____

❧

Just as no one can know the day or the hour when the end-times events will begin, so also the identities of the two key combatants will be hidden until the time comes for them to be revealed (2 Thessalonians 2:7–8). Until that moment, however, we must continue to contend with the various means of spiritual deception already at work in the world. Each of us must commit to equip ourselves for spiritual battle with the knowledge, discernment, and wisdom that come only from the Father, Son, and Holy Spirit through the revelation of God's perfect Word. Are you equipped to face the challenges of today's earthly drama with heavenly power?

HOW TO BEGIN A RELATIONSHIP WITH GOD

Many people associate the book of Revelation with visions of fire and brimstone, but sometimes they forget that Revelation is filled with profound promises. To those who "overcome," Christ personally offers eternal life, a guaranteed inheritance, the prospects of reigning as royalty over the earth, and freedom from suffering, sorrow, and death (Revelation 2:7, 11, 17, 26; 3:5, 12, 21). Who are the ones who "overcome?" Are they super-saints who live unblemished lives? Do they work hard enough to earn their own reward? Have they suffered and died for the faith? Do they attend the right church and go through the right rituals? The apostle John makes clear who these victorious ones really are: "Who is the one who overcomes the world, but he who believes that Jesus is the Son of God?" (1 John 5:5).

To understand how you can begin a relationship with God and join the number of those who "overcome," we need to back up from the end of the story and consider the beginning. The most marvelous book in the world, the Bible, marks the path to God with four vital truths. Let's look at each marker in detail.

OUR SPIRITUAL CONDITION: TOTALLY DEPRAVED

The first truth is rather personal. One look in the mirror of Scripture, and our human condition becomes painfully clear:

> There is none righteous, not even one;
> There is none who understands,
> There is none who seeks for God;
> All have turned aside, together they have become useless;
> There is none who does good,
> There is not even one. (Romans 3:10–12)

We are all sinners through and through—totally depraved. Now, that doesn't mean we've committed every atrocity known to humankind. We're not as *bad* as we can be, just as *bad off* as we can be. Sin colors all our thoughts, motives, words, and actions.

You still don't believe it? Look around. Everything around us bears the smudge marks of our sinful nature. Despite our best efforts to create a perfect world, crime statistics continue to soar, divorce rates keep climbing, and families keep crumbling.

Something has gone terribly wrong in our society and in ourselves—something deadly. Contrary to how the world would repackage it, "me-first" living doesn't equal rugged individuality and freedom; it equals death. As Paul said in his letter to the Romans, "The wages of sin is death" (Romans 6:23)—our spiritual and physical death that comes from God's righteous judgment of our sin, along with all of the emotional and practical effects of this separation that we experience on a daily basis. This brings us to the second marker: God's character.

GOD'S CHARACTER: INFINITELY HOLY

How can a good God judge the world with the wrath described in Revelation? To bring it closer to home, how can God judge each of us for a sinful state we were born into? Our total depravity is only half the answer. The other half is God's infinite holiness.

The fact that we know things are not as they should be points us to a standard of goodness beyond ourselves. Our sense of injustice in life on this side of eternity implies a perfect standard of justice beyond our reality. That standard and source is God Himself. And God's standard of holiness contrasts starkly with our sinful condition.

Scripture says that "God is Light, and in Him there is no darkness at all" (1 John 1:5). He is absolutely holy—which creates a problem for us. If He is so pure, how can we who are so impure relate to Him?

Perhaps we could try being better people, try to tilt the balance in favor of our good deeds, or seek out methods for self-improvement. Throughout history, people have attempted to live up to God's standard by keeping the Ten Commandments or living by their own code of ethics. Unfortunately, no one can come close to satisfying the demands of God's law. Romans 3:20 says, "For no one can ever be made right in God's sight by doing what his law commands. For the more we know God's law, the clearer it becomes that we aren't obeying it" (NLT).

OUR NEED: A SUBSTITUTE

So here we are, sinners by nature and sinners by choice, trying to pull ourselves up by our own bootstraps to attain a relationship with our holy Creator. But every time we try, we fall flat on our faces. We can't live a life that's good enough to make up for our sin, because God's standard isn't "good enough"—it's *perfection*. And we can't make amends for the offense our sin has created without dying for it.

Who can get us out of this mess?

If someone could live perfectly, honoring God's law, and would bear sin's death penalty for us—in our place—then we would be saved from our predicament. But is there such a person? Thankfully, yes!

Meet your substitute—*Jesus Christ*. He is the One who took death's place for you!

> [God] made [Jesus Christ] who knew no sin to be sin on our behalf, so that we might become the righteousness of God in Him. (2 Corinthians 5:21)

GOD'S PROVISION: A SAVIOR

God rescued us by sending His Son, Jesus, to die for our sins on the cross (1 John 4:9–10). Jesus was fully human and fully divine (John 1:1, 18), a truth that ensures His understanding of our weaknesses, His power to forgive, and His ability to bridge the gap between God and us (Romans 5:6–11). In short, we are "justified as a gift by His grace through the redemption which is in Christ Jesus" (Romans 3:24). Two words in this verse bear further explanation: *justified* and *redemption*.

Justification is God's act of mercy, in which He declares believing sinners righteous while they are still in their sinning state. Justification doesn't mean that God *makes* us righteous, so that we never sin again, but rather that He *declares* us righteous—much like a judge pardons a guilty criminal. Because Jesus took our sin upon Himself and suffered our judgment on the cross, God forgives our debt and proclaims us PARDONED.

Redemption is God's act of paying the ransom price to release us from our bondage to sin. Held hostage by Satan, we were shackled by the iron chains of sin and death. Like a loving parent whose child has been kidnapped, God willingly paid the ransom for you. And what a price He paid! He gave His only Son to bear our sins—past, present, and future. Jesus's death and resurrection broke our chains and set us free to become children of God (Romans 6:16–18, 22; Galatians 4:4–7).

PLACING YOUR FAITH IN CHRIST

These four truths describe how God has provided a way to Himself through Jesus Christ. Because the price has been paid in full by God, we must respond to His free gift of eternal life in total faith and confidence in Him to save us. We must step forward into the relationship with God that He has prepared for us—not by doing good works or being a good person, but by coming to Him just as we are and accepting His justification and redemption by faith.

> For by grace you have been saved through faith; and that not of your-selves, it is the gift of God; not as a result of works, so that no one may boast. (Ephesians 2:8–9)

We accept God's gift of salvation simply by placing our faith in Christ alone for the forgiveness of our sins. Would you like to enter a relationship with your Creator by trusting in Christ as your Savior? If so, here's a simple prayer you can use to express your faith:

> *Dear God,*
>
> *I know that my sin has put a barrier between You and me. Thank You for sending Your Son, Jesus, to die in my place. I trust in Jesus alone to forgive my sins, and I accept His gift of eternal life. I ask Jesus to be my personal Savior and the Lord of my life. Thank You.*
>
> *In Jesus's name, amen.*

If you've prayed this prayer or one like it and you wish to find out more about knowing God and His plan for you in the Bible, contact us using the information below.

Pastoral Ministries Department
Insight for Living
Post Office Box 269000
Plano, Texas 75026-9000
USA
972-473-5097
www.insight.org/contactapastor

ENDNOTES

LESSON ONE

Unless otherwise noted below, all material in this chapter is adapted from "Let the Judgments Begin," a sermon by Charles R. Swindoll, and supplemented by the Creative Ministries department of Insight for Living.

1. Robert A. Pyne, "Humanity and Sin," in *Understanding Christian Theology*, ed. Charles R. Swindoll and Roy B. Zuck (Nashville: Thomas Nelson, 2003), 758.

2. Walter Bauer and others, eds., *A Greek-English Lexicon of the New Testament and Other Early Christian Literature*, 2d rev. ed. (Chicago: University of Chicago Press, 1979), 767.

3. Grant R. Osborne, *Revelation*, Baker Exegetical Commentary on the New Testament, ed. Moisés Silva (Grand Rapids: Baker Academic, 2002), 278.

4. G. K. Beale, *The Book of Revelation: A Commentary on the Greek Text*, The New International Greek Testament Commentary, ed. I. Howard Marshall and Donald A. Hagner (Grand Rapids: Wm. B. Eerdmans Publishing Co., 1999), 381. Used by permission.

5. Bauer and others, eds., *A Greek-English Lexicon of the New Testament and Other Early Christian Literature*, 882.

LESSON TWO

Unless otherwise noted below, all material in this chapter is adapted from "More Seals Broken . . . More Lives Shaken and Taken," a sermon by Charles R. Swindoll, and supplemented by the Creative Ministries department of Insight for Living.

1. Walter Bauer and others, eds., *A Greek-English Lexicon of the New Testament and Other Early Christian Literature*, 2d rev. ed. (Chicago: University of Chicago Press, 1979), 769.

2. Geza Vermes, ed., *The Complete Dead Sea Scrolls in English* (New York: Penguin Books, 1997), 102.

3. For a brief discussion of the timing of the church's rapture to heaven, see *Revelation—Unveiling the End, Act 1: The Heavenly Stage*, Lesson 9.

4 Alan Johnson, "Revelation," in *The Expositor's Bible Commentary*, vol. 12, *Hebrews—Revelation*, ed. Frank E. Gaebelein and J. D. Douglas (Grand Rapids: Zondervan, 1981), 476.

5. John F. Walvoord, "Revelation," in *The Bible Knowledge Commentary: New Testament Edition*, ed. John F. Walvoord and Roy B. Zuck (Wheaton, Ill.: Victor Books, 1983), 949. © 1983 by Zuck and Walvoord. Reprinted with permission by Cook Communications Ministries. May not be further reproduced. To order, www.cookministries.com. All rights reserved.

LESSON THREE

Unless otherwise noted below, all material in this chapter is adapted from "An Interlude: Earthly Restraint and Heavenly Worship," a sermon by Charles R. Swindoll, and supplemented by the Creative Ministries department of Insight for Living.

1. Alan Johnson, "Revelation," in *The Expositor's Bible Commentary*, vol. 12, *Hebrews—Revelation*, ed. Frank E. Gaebelein and J. D. Douglas (Grand Rapids: Zondervan, 1981), 482.

2. For some explanations on these differences, see John F. Walvoord, "Revelation," in *The Bible Knowledge Commentary: New Testament Edition*, ed. John F. Walvoord and Roy B. Zuck (Wheaton, Ill.: Victor Books, 1983), 949.

3. Walvoord, "Revelation," 949. © 1983 by Zuck and Walvoord. Reprinted with permission by Cook Communications Ministries. May not be further reproduced. To order, www.cookministries.com. All rights reserved.

LESSON FOUR

Unless otherwise noted below, all material in this chapter is adapted from "First Blasts of the Trumpet Plagues," a sermon by Charles R. Swindoll, and supplemented by the Creative Ministries department of Insight for Living.

1. C. S. Lewis, *The Problem of Pain*, paperback ed. (New York: Macmillan, 1962; reprint, New York: Macmillan, 1986), 93.

2. For the various uses of the trumpet in the Old and New Testaments, see Grant R. Osborne, *Revelation*, Baker Exegetical Commentary on the New Testament, ed. Moisés Silva (Grand Rapids: Baker Academic, 2002), 342–43.

3. J. D. Douglas and Merrill C. Tenney, eds., *The New International Dictionary of the Bible*, pictorial ed. (Grand Rapids: Zondervan, 1987), 465.

4. Douglas and Tenney, eds., *The New International Dictionary of the Bible*, 806.

5. John Phillips, *Exploring Revelation*, rev. ed. (Chicago: Moody Press, 1987), 118. Used by permission.

6. Phillips, *Exploring Revelation*, 118. Used by permission.

7. Robert P. Lightner, "Angels, Satan, and Demons," in *Understanding Christian Theology*, ed. Charles R. Swindoll and Roy B. Zuck (Nashville: Thomas Nelson, 2003), 537–640.

LESSON FIVE

Unless otherwise noted below, all material in this chapter is adapted from "A Glance Back to the Future," a sermon by Charles R. Swindoll, and supplemented by the Creative Ministries department of Insight for Living.

1. For further study of this vision, see *Revelation—Unveiling the End, Act 1: The Heavenly Stage Bible Companio*n, lesson one.

2. To study all of the messages to these churches in more detail, see *Revelation— Unveiling the End, Act 1: The Heavenly Stage Bible Companion*, lessons four through ten.

LESSON SIX

Unless otherwise noted below, all material in this chapter is adapted from "Releasing Demons from the Abyss," a sermon by Charles R. Swindoll, and supplemented by the Creative Ministries department of Insight for Living.

1. John F. Walvoord, "Revelation," in *The Bible Knowledge Commentary, New Testament Edition*, ed. John F. Walvoord and Roy B. Zuck (Wheaton, Ill.: Victor Books, 1983), 952.

2. Walter Bauer and others, eds., *A Greek-English Lexicon of the New Testament and Other Early Christian Literature*, 2d rev. ed. (Chicago: University of Chicago Press, 1979), 2.

3. Charles C. Ryrie, *Basic Theology* (Chicago: Moody Publishers, 1999), 187. Used by permission.

4. G. L. Keown, "Locust," in *The International Standard Bible Encyclopedia*, vol. 3, *K–P*, rev. ed., ed. Geoffrey W. Bromiley and others (Grand Rapids: Wm. B. Eerdmans, 1986), 150.

5. B. C. Birch, "Scorpion," in *The International Standard Bible Encyclopedia*, vol. 4, *Q–Z*, rev. ed., ed. Geoffrey W. Bromiley and others (Grand Rapids: Wm. B. Eerdmans, 1988), 358.

6. "Animals," in *The New International Dictionary of the Bible*, ed. J. D. Douglas and Merrill C. Tenney (Grand Rapids: Zondervan, 1987), 56.

7. Grant R. Osborne, *Revelation*, Baker Exegetical Commentary on the New Testament, ed. Moisés Silva (Grand Rapids: Baker Academic, 2002), 373.

Lesson Seven

Unless otherwise noted below, all material in this chapter is adapted from "More Demons, More Death, More Defiance," a sermon by Charles R. Swindoll, and supplemented by the Creative Ministries department of Insight for Living.

1. Grant R. Osborne, *Revelation*, Baker Exegetical Commentary on the New Testament, ed. Moisés Silva (Grand Rapids: Baker Academic, 2002), 388.

2. J. A. Seiss, *The Apocalypse: Lectures on the Book of Revelation*, 6th reprint ed. (Grand Rapids: Zondervan, 1966), 221.

3. Donald Grey Barnhouse, *Revelation: An Expositional Commentary* (Grand Rapids: Zondervan, 1971), 177.

4. Paul Leslie Garber, "Idolatry," in *The International Standard Bible Encyclopedia*, vol. 2, *E–J*, ed. Geoffrey W. Bromiley and others (Grand Rapids: Wm. B. Eerdmans, 1982), 799.

5. Steven Barabas, "Idolatry," in *The New International Dictionary of the Bible*, pictorial ed., ed. J. D. Douglas and Merrill C. Tenney (Grand Rapids: Zondervan, 1987), 461.

LESSON EIGHT

Unless otherwise noted below, all material in this chapter is adapted from "A Strong Angel, a Strange Assignment," a sermon by Charles R. Swindoll, and supplemented by the Creative Ministries department of Insight for Living.

1. John Eldredge, *Waking the Dead: The Glory of a Heart Fully Alive* (Nashville: Nelson Books, 2003), 26–34.

2. John F. Walvoord, "Revelation," in *The Bible Knowledge Commentary, New Testament Edition*, ed. John F. Walvoord and Roy B. Zuck (Wheaton, Ill.: Victor Books, 1983), 954. © 1983 by Zuck and Walvoord. Reprinted with permission by Cook Communications Ministries. May not be further reproduced. To order, www.cookministries.com. All rights reserved.

3. G. K. Beale, *The Book of Revelation: A Commentary on the Greek Text*, The New International Greek Testament Commentary, ed. I. Howard Marshall and Donald A. Hagner (Grand Rapids: Wm. B. Eerdmans Publishing Co., 1999), 551. Used by permission.

LESSON NINE

Unless otherwise noted below, all material in this chapter is adapted from "Two Fearless, Future Witnesses," a sermon by Charles R. Swindoll, and supplemented by the Creative Ministries department of Insight for Living.

1. Charles C. Ryrie, *The Ryrie Study Bible: New International Version*, expanded ed. (Chicago: Moody Press, 1994), 1961.

2. G. K. Beale, *The Book of Revelation: A Commentary on the Greek Text*, The New International Greek Testament Commentary, ed. I. Howard Marshall and Donald A. Hagner (Grand Rapids: Wm. B. Eerdmans Publishing Co., 1999), 572–73; Grant R. Osborne, *Revelation*, Baker Exegetical Commentary on the New Testament, ed. Moisés Silva (Grand Rapids: Baker Academic, 2002), 417–18.

3. Commentators disagree on whether these two witnesses prophesy during the first half, second half, or middle of the seven-year tribulation. Ryrie suggests that this refers to the first half of the tribulation, while Walvoord says it refers to the second. In the end, one's view on this matter does not affect the practical implications of this passage. We are probably better off suspending judgment on this matter. See Charles C. Ryrie, *The Ryrie Study Bible: New International Version*, expanded ed. (Chicago: Moody Press, 1994), 1961; John F. Walvoord, *The Prophecy Knowledge Handbook* (Wheaton, Ill.: Victor Books, 1990), 573–75.

4. Osborne, *Revelation*, 418.

Lesson Ten

Unless otherwise noted below, all material in this chapter is adapted from "The Sounding of the Seventh Trumpet," a sermon by Charles R. Swindoll, and supplemented by the Creative Ministries department of Insight for Living.

1. The Didache, one of the earliest Christian writings outside the New Testament, instructs believers to pray a prayer like the Lord's Prayer three times every day (Didache 8.2–3).

2. John F. Walvoord, "Revelation," in *The Bible Knowledge Commentary, New Testament Edition*, ed. John F. Walvoord and Roy B. Zuck (Wheaton, Ill.: Victor Books, 1983), 956–57. © 1983 by Zuck and Walvoord. Reprinted with permission by Cook Communications Ministries. May not be further reproduced. To order, www.cookministries.com. All rights reserved.

3. S. R. Driver, *A Treatise on the Use of the Tenses in Hebrew and Some Other Syntactical Questions*, 3d rev. ed. (Oxford: Oxford University Press, 1892; reprint, Oxford: Oxford University Press, 1969), 18.

LESSON ELEVEN

Unless otherwise noted below, all material in this chapter is adapted from "Exposing the Ultimate Evil Empire," a sermon by Charles R. Swindoll, and supplemented by the Creative Ministries department of Insight for Living.

1. C. S. Lewis, *The Screwtape Letters* (New York: Macmillan, 1961), 3.

2. John F. Walvoord, "Revelation," in *The Bible Knowledge Commentary, New Testament Edition*, ed. John F. Walvoord and Roy B. Zuck (Wheaton, Ill.: Victor Books, 1983), 959. © 1983 by Zuck and Walvoord. Reprinted with permission by Cook Communications Ministries. May not be further reproduced. To order, www.cookministries.com. All rights reserved.

LESSON TWELVE

Unless otherwise noted below, all material in this chapter is adapted from "Antichrist: The Beast Out of the Sea," a sermon by Charles R. Swindoll, and supplemented by the Creative Ministries department of Insight for Living.

1. J. Dwight Pentecost, "Daniel," in *The Bible Knowledge Commentary: Old Testament Edition*, ed. John F. Walvoord and Roy B. Zuck (Wheaton, Ill.: Victor Books, 1985), 1350–1355.

2. John F. Walvoord, "Revelation," in *The Bible Knowledge Commentary: New Testament Edition*, ed. John F. Walvoord and Roy B. Zuck (Wheaton, Ill.: Victor Books, 1983), 960. © 1983 by Zuck and Walvoord. Reprinted with permission by Cook Communications Ministries. May not be further reproduced. To order, www.cookministries.com. All rights reserved.

3. For a discussion of the variety of interpretations of the "fatal wound," see Grant R. Osborne, *Revelation*, Baker Exegetical Commentary on the New Testament, ed. Moisés Silva (Grand Rapids: Baker Academic, 2002), 495–97 and John F. Walvoord, *The Prophecy Knowledge Handbook* (Wheaton, Ill.: Victor Books, 1990), 582–583.

LESSON THIRTEEN

Unless otherwise noted below, all material in this chapter is adapted from "Antichrist's Lieutenant: The Beast Out of the Earth," a sermon by Charles R. Swindoll, and supplemented by the Creative Ministries department of Insight for Living.

1. Grant R. Osborne, *Revelation*, Baker Exegetical Commentary on the New Testament, ed. Moisés Silva (Grand Rapids: Baker Academic, 2002), 591.

2. Walter Bauer and others, eds., *A Greek-English Lexicon of the New Testament and Other Early Christian Literature*, 2d rev. ed. (Chicago: University of Chicago Press, 1979), 665.

3. John Phillips, *Exploring Revelation*, rev. ed. (Chicago: Moody Press, 1987), 171. Used by permission.

4. Osborne, *Revelation*, 519.

5. *Merriam-Webster's Collegiate Dictionary*, 11th ed. (Springfield, Mass.: Merriam-Webster, 2003), see "discernment."

RESOURCES FOR PROBING FURTHER

For those who want to probe further into God's plan for the future, we recommend the following books written or edited by Bible-believing scholars.

GENERAL WORKS ON THE END TIMES

Benware, Paul N. *Understanding End Times Prophecy: A Comprehensive Approach*. Chicago: Moody, 1995.

Peterson, Eugene H. *Reversed Thunder: The Revelation of John and the Praying Imagination*. San Francisco: HarperSanFrancisco, 1988.

Swindoll, Charles R., J. Dwight Pentecost, and John F. Walvoord. *The Road to Armageddon: A Biblical Understanding of Prophecy and End Time Events*. Nashville: Word, 1999.

Walvoord, John F. *End Times: Understanding Today's World Events in Biblical Prophecy*. Swindoll Leadership Library, ed. Charles R. Swindoll. Dallas: Word, 1998.

Zuck, Roy B., ed. *Vital Prophetic Issues: Examining Promises and Problems in Eschatology*. Grand Rapids: Kregel, 1995.

COMMENTARIES AND REFERENCE WORKS ON THE BOOK OF REVELATION

Couch, Mal, ed. *A Bible Handbook to Revelation*. Grand Rapids: Kregel, 2001.

Ryrie, Charles C. *Revelation*. New ed. Everyman's Bible Commentary. Chicago: Moody, 1996.

Stedman, Ray C., and James D. Denney. *God's Final Word: Understanding Revelation*. Grand Rapids: Discovery House, 1991.

Thomas, Robert L. *Revelation 1–7: An Exegetical Commentary*. Ed. Kenneth Barker and Moisés Silva. Chicago: Moody, 1992.

Thomas, Robert L. *Revelation 8–22: An Exegetical Commentary*. Ed. Kenneth Barker and Moisés Silva. Chicago: Moody, 1995.

Walvoord, John F. *The Revelation of Jesus Christ*. Chicago: Moody, 1966.

DIFFERING VIEWS ON REVELATION AND THE END TIMES

Archer, Gleason L., Jr., ed. *Three Views on the Rapture: Pre-, Mid-, or Post-Tribulation*. Grand Rapids: Zondervan, 1996.

Bock, Darrell L., ed. *Three Views on the Millennium and Beyond*. Grand Rapids: Zondervan 1999.

Erickson, Millard J. *A Basic Guide to Eschatology: Making Sense of the Millennium*. Rev. ed. Grand Rapids: Baker Book House, 1998.

Pate, C. Marvin., ed. *Four Views on the Book of Revelation*. Grand Rapids: Zondervan, 1998.

ORDERING INFORMATION

If you would like to order additional copies of *Revelation — Unveiling the End, Act 2, The Earthly Drama* or order other Insight for Living resources, please contact the office that serves you.

United States

Insight for Living
Post Office Box 269000
Plano, Texas 75026-9000
USA
1-800-772-8888,
Monday through Thursday
7:00 a.m. – 9:00 p.m. and
Friday 7:00 a.m. – 7:00 p.m.
Central time
www.insight.org

Canada

Insight for Living Canada
Post Office Box 2510
Vancouver, BC V6B 3W7
CANADA
1-800-663-7639
www.insightforliving.ca

Australia, New Zealand, and South Pacific

Insight for Living Australia
Post Office Box 1011
Bayswater, VIC 3153
AUSTRALIA
1300 467 444
www.insight.asn.au

United Kingdom and Europe

Insight for Living United Kingdom
Post Office Box 348
Leatherhead
KT22 2DS
UNITED KINGDOM
0800 915 9364
www.insightforliving.org.uk

Other International Locations

International constituents may contact the U.S. office through our Web site (www.insight.org), mail queries, or by calling +1-972-473-5136.

NOTES

NOTES

NOTES

NOTES